GOD'S RELENTLESS LOVE

Tiger Iron Press

Macon, Georgia, USA

GOD'S RELENTLESS LOVE

EDWIN CHASE

Tiger Iron Press

http://www.TigerIronPress.com

LIBRARY OF CONGRESS CATALOGING – IN – PUBLICATION DATA

Includes endnotes and bibliography
God's Relentless Love / Edwin Chase
ISBN 978-0-9787263-7-9
1. Christian life. 2. Love (Theology) 3. Image of God

First Edition: January, 2011

DEDICATION

To Carole,
from whom I have learned of
courage, loyalty and love.

And to our sons,
David, Danny and Michael,
who filled our home
with laughter, wonder and joy.

TABLE OF CONTENTS

<u>CHAPTERS</u>

RESOURCES AND RECOGNITIONS

PREFACE

We have a God whose wondrous love is more gracious, kind and remarkable than we can imagine or words can express. When Isaiah proclaims: "What eye has not seen, nor has ear heard, nor has entered the heart of man what God has prepared..." (Isaiah 64:4; 1 Corinthians 2:9), Isaiah is simply saying that God has taken pains to prepare *an unspeakable surprise.* Who is this God who takes us unaware and at times leaves us speechless?

It is the same relentless God who interrupts the prayers of Daniel *three times* to tell him he is beloved. There is something so likable about a Savior in Galilee who is the *toast of the town,* who turns water into wine and becomes the *talk of the town.* We are astounded by the savvy, courage and compassion of a Savior, who simply by writing in the sand and re-directing an angry mob, saves the life of a terrified woman. There is something inspiring and endearing about a Savior who tells a parable of a lost sheep, a lost coin and a lost son – because the parable is about God, who of all things – *goes searching for us!* And when we are found, the Savior calls for a party to rejoice over us. Who wouldn't want to know such a God as this?

Tragically, this compelling picture of an awesome Savior who takes us by surprise has been lost. Over the centuries the picture of a gracious God has been distorted as remnants of the old Protestant work ethic and images from the sermon, "Sinners in the Hands of an Angry God" are in the very air we breathe. Because of this distortion, God is seen as demanding and harsh, thundering in the distance – a taskmaster who cannot be satisfied.

But every now and then a magnificent and winsome God reveals to us an unexpected and delightful side. That is what this book is all about. In scripture and in our everyday lives we will catch a glimpse of a remarkable God whose mirth makes us laugh out loud and whose kindness takes our breath away. Who is this God that does the most outlandish things with the most unlikely people? We are promised that one day we will see God face to face. In the meantime, God continues to catch us off guard by a startling act of mercy or a mind-boggling "coincidence."

But will you see it when it happens?

This book is an invitation to see God in new ways and allow a fresh picture of a surprisingly likable God to change your life.

INTRODUCTION

In the pages that follow, you are invited to encounter a God who loves you and delights over you. Because all good theology begins with God, a biblical underpinning for God's relentless love will reveal a rich reservoir of metaphors and narratives portraying a remarkable God whose love can be experienced in your everyday life.

What is meant when God's love is described as relentless? The word *relent* comes from two Latin words: *re*, meaning "back," and *lentus* meaning pliant or flexible. When the suffix "less" is added, it means unbending or resolute. When God's love is described as relentless, it means the Creator's love is persistent, unwavering, coming toward you again and again in different ways.

The Apostle Paul captures the persistence of God's love in a single verse in First Corinthians. One of the most familiar lines found in scripture, verse seven, is more than beautiful prose; it's an eloquent expression of God's love.

After listing what love would *never* do, Paul gives a short list of love's perpetual endeavors:

> Love bears all things,
>   Believes all things,
>   Hopes all things,
>   Endures all things (1 Corinthians 13:7).

Love has the enormous capacity to bear *all things*: the sting of rejection, the agony of betrayal, the anguish of a bitter disappointment or the pain of a deep sadness. These are some of the harsh realities that love can withstand. It's an extraordinary claim. And if it's true, we need to ask what enables love to carry such a heavy weight, to bear up under such a burden? What is love's secret? After stating that love bears all things, Paul uses the next few lines to explain *how* love carries off this remarkable feat. Described in three simple assertions, he states that love

> Believes all things,
>   Hopes all things,
>   Endures all things.

For those who read Greek, the rhythm and cadence of the parallel structure add emphasis and power:

> *panta pisteuei,*
>   *panta elpigei,*
>   *panta upomenei.*

We often use *panta* in everyday English. *Panorama* is the ability to see all things. *Pantheism* is the belief that God is in all things. *Panacea* is the cure for all things. *Panta* means "all things." Paul repeats the word *panta* to accentuate "all things" because God's love has the innate capacity to respond to *all* situations, *all* possibilities.

Regardless of your circumstance in life, God's love is relentless as it never gives up, reaching out to you in three gracious initiatives – *believing, hoping and enduring.* Always changing in its form, God's love becomes what is most needed in the present moment. God's love believes all things concerning you, hopes all things for you and endures all things with you.

GOD'S RELENTLESS LOVE

Chapter One

LOVE ALWAYS BELIEVES THE BEST

"Treat people as if they were what they ought to be, and you help them to become what they are capable of being."
—*Johann Wolfgang von Goethe*

Love Believes All Things

Love believes all things means that it believes the best in you despite all evidence to the contrary. It believes the best in people and circumstances. The first time you meet someone, you can choose to think highly of that person or you can judge the person as dull, lazy or boring. But love always aims high; a new acquaintance is always highly regarded. In this way love believes all things concerning *everyone.*

In John's Gospel Jesus presents a compelling picture of what can happen when someone dares to believe the best in a situation where most people would believe the worst. While Jesus was teaching near the temple in Jerusalem, He was interrupted by a group of scribes and Pharisees who wanted to trap Him. They brought before Him a woman who had been caught in adultery and set her in the middle of an accusing circle. All eyes were upon her. The leaders said to Jesus: "Now in the law Moses commanded us to stone such. What do you say about her" (John 8:5)?

Even though Jesus knew He was being set up so that the scribes and Pharisees could bring a charge against Him, He chose to believe the best regarding *everyone* involved. Without saying a word, Jesus did the unexpected: He knelt down and began writing in the sand. We don't know what He wrote. Some say Jesus wrote the law, "You shall not commit adultery." Others have suggested He wrote the sins of the onlookers or possibly the names of *their* girlfriends.

Regardless of what He wrote, Jesus believed the unruly crowd would read what He had written. Then He stood and addressed those with stones in their hands:

"Let him who is without sin among you be the first to throw a stone at her" (8:7).

Now the onlookers are looking within themselves.

Despite the surly mood of the crowd, Jesus believed the best concerning them. He believed that they would take to heart His moral challenge. And they did. Slowly the crowd dispersed, and Jesus was left alone with the terrified woman. He asked her, "Woman, where are they? Has no one condemned you?"

"No one, Lord."

"Neither do I condemn you; go, and do not sin again" (8:10-11).

Jesus chose to believe the best about this woman despite her shameful circumstance. In doing so, love was released to do its redemptive work. In His final words to her that she should not sin again, it is clear that Jesus *expected* her not to sin again. In this powerful affirmation He told her to go and live a new life. He believed *in* her and believed the best *for* her.

Amazingly, Jesus believed the best concerning all the players in the drama that unfolded that day near the steps of the temple. Had He not believed the way He did, the sequence of events may have led to a tragic conclusion. Jesus' love was both daring and kind. He moved swiftly to shift the focus of the crowd away from the woman's sin and onto the sins of those carrying the stones. With an economy of words and action, Jesus changed the story line from one of condemnation and death to one of forgiveness and new life.

This Gospel story of "love in action" challenges us – regardless of the circumstances – to believe the best in others with reckless abandon.

Seeing Beyond Appearances

When Kristen Johnson Ingram saw a "grizzled man" standing on a freeway exit holding a sign that read, "Work for Food," she slowed down and handed him some money and drove on. Her friend in the passenger seat lost no time castigating her, telling her the man would probably spend the money on wine, cigarettes or drugs. When Ingram was told that she should only give her money to reputable agencies, she responded by reminding her critic what Jesus said in the Gospel of Matthew: "Give to anyone who asks you, and if anyone wants to borrow, do not turn away" (Matthew 5:42 NJB).

At another time, while Ingram was waiting for a cab on Dupont Circle in Washington, D.C., a man asked her for money to buy food, and she gave him a twenty dollar bill. Having just visited the ATM machine, she had nothing smaller. When the man asked if she had intended to give him just a dollar bill, she said, "No." And he walked off yelling, "Thaaaannk you, Jesus!"

For Kristen Johnson Ingram, "Caring for others, whether they are poor or depressed or confused, is to perceive the extraordinary in the ordinary, to let your imagination soar." She believes all things for the people she encounters on the streets. Some people would accuse her of being naïve; and they would be correct. However, the alternative would be to judge the poor and homeless by their appearance. Ingram asks, "Do we decide by their looks or demeanor that they aren't qualified for our caring?" No. It is because love believes all things concerning the poor, the confused, and the homeless. Love always reaches out with a helping hand. This is the way of God's love. Regardless of how someone may appear, he or she always qualifies for God's love that cares with the tenderness of a mother for her child.

Love Can Stop Evil in Its Tracks

When we believe all things about a person despite the evidence, now and then we catch a glimpse of love's enormous power. On April 11, 2005, Brian Nichols, in custody on a rape charge, overpowered his guards and escaped from the Fulton County Courthouse in Atlanta, and before it was over, he had killed four people. While still on the loose, he took Ashley Smith, a thirty-year-old divorcee, captive and forced her to take him to her apartment.

Although Ashley Smith was his captive, she chose to believe all things concerning Nichols. By her account, she talked with him, shared her own story of loss, and made him breakfast. As his prisoner, she welcomed him to her table and read excerpts to him from *The Purpose Driven Life*.

I am convinced that her hospitality, her unexpected and surprising acts of kindness broke evil's powerful hold on Nichols and prevented further violence. Such is the power of believing all things about someone.

When all the facts were warning Ashley Smith that she should believe nothing good about the fugitive who held her hostage, she extended to him the grace of God. As I ponder this act of kindness to a criminal, another criminal comes to mind.

In *Les Misérables* Victor Hugo tells the tale of a bishop who dared to believe all things concerning a convicted thief. This extraordinary bishop held a unique perspective. He believed that if souls were left in darkness, without education or Christian instruction, sins would be committed. For the bishop, the guilty one is not the person who commits the sin, but the one who causes the darkness. Therefore, this bishop always reached out to the poor and needy.

Following Jean Valjean's release from prison for stealing a loaf of bread, he wandered across France. Door after door was slammed in his face until he arrived at the bishop's home. There, to his astonishment, Valjean was invited to enter, to eat supper and to spend the night. At dinner, Valjean spied the exquisite silver pieces and devised a plan. When everyone was asleep, he would steal them. And under the cloak of darkness, he did just that. However, he was caught by the police, searched, and taken back to the bishop's residence.

The bishop's response was totally unexpected. Unthinkable! He explained to the officers that he had given Valjean the silver plates as a gift. He then turned to Valjean and told him how glad he was that he had returned and chided him for not taking the most valuable of all the pieces – the silver candlesticks.

The bishop then stuffed the candlesticks into Valjean's knapsack, instantly making him a wealthy man. And after the police had departed, in a low voice the bishop whispered to Valjean:

"Forget not, never forget that you have promised me to use this silver to become an honest man." Then, emphasizing each word, the bishop whispered, "Jean Valjean, my brother, you no longer belong to evil, but to good. It is your soul that I am buying for you."

This extraordinary act of love transformed Valjean's life. Slowly, over time, his life was changed as he began to show kindness to others, not unlike what the bishop had shown him.

Again, an unexpected act of love defeats the forces of evil. Despite all the evidence that Valjean was nothing but a thief, the bishop saw in him so much more and persisted in believing all things concerning him. The bishop's gamble paid off. Years later Jean Valjean emerged as a hardworking and generous man.

Victor Hugo's story and Ashley Smith's experience illustrate the power of love to thwart the power of evil. St. Peter, in one of his pastoral epistles, offers an insight into love's power: "For love covers a multitude of sins" (1 Peter 4:8).

Peter is not referring to "a cover up" like we might read about in the newspaper. He paints a picture of love surrounding and blocking the multiplicity of sins. The nature of sin is to spread like leaven in a loaf. The Greek word for covers is *kalupe,* which means to surround and cut off, to stop the multiplying process. In this way love "covers" or encapsulates evil. When we believe all things concerning those who cross our path, it releases love's power to stop the accelerating advance of evil.

Søren Kierkegaard, a nineteenth century Danish theologian, in *Works of Love* explains *how* love covers a multitude of sin. For Kierkegaard, love does this in three ways. First, concerning a neighbor's sin, love *keeps silent.* Love does not talk about the sin of another person. To talk about another person's sin is to increase it. For Kierkegaard, "Love hides the multiplicity of sin in silence." There is a natural inclination to want to talk about the sins of others, but love chooses to remain silent, and in this way stops the multiplying process. There are times, of course, when love chooses to talk about sin but does so in a redemptive manner, not in a careless way.

Secondly, love covers sin with *a mitigating explanation.* In short, love looks for the best excuse. Let's say someone intentionally bumps into me on the street knocking me off balance. If I say it was an accident, my mitigating explanation nullifies the sin. When love chooses not to acknowledge the sin, for all practical purposes it goes away.

Third, love covers sin by *forgiving it*. When forgiven, sin is blotted out, removed, or washed away. In the gracious act of forgiveness the victim chooses not to hold the sin against the perpetrator. Scripture teaches that when God forgives, God hides the sin behind His back (Isaiah 38:17). The one sinned against chooses not to remember the sin against the offender. In these practical ways, love stops evil in its tracks.

Go Ahead and Jump!

Believing all things is more than just thinking about a matter; it is putting what you believe into practice. Albert Einstein once said, "Nothing happens unless something moves." If you really believe, sometimes it means you take action without absolute certainty. I witnessed an example of this several years ago off the coast of Scotland. Every year on Staffa Island a drama takes place that illustrates the relationship between belief and action.

Staffa is the home of hundreds of seabirds that nest in its lofty grasslands. From June to early August the puffins hatch their young and teach them to fly. These birds, looking more like little wide-eyed penguins with orange beaks and legs, practice flying 200 feet above the water's surface. With nothing but their wings and their instinct to fly, the fledglings flap their wings and for the first time leap off into thin air. And fly they do, making a large circle and returning only long enough to catch their breath and do it all over again. And if you sit in the grass close to the cliff, the puffins will nestle in the tall grass at your feet. The daring puffins in their first days of flight school are a perfect picture of taking action with no guarantees. These birds do more than look at the water far below; they leap off into the sky with no certainty that their efforts will succeed.

Of course the puffins don't "decide" to jump; they do it instinctively. But their temerity is impressive. The temptation is to stand on the edge of a new venture and do *nothing*. Just stand there. Before I started writing for journals, magazines and a newspaper, I knew I had something to say but was afraid I would not be taken seriously. This fear kept me paralyzed for many years. I just stood there thinking about it. Then I happened upon a quote from Carl Jung that set me free. These lines from Jung

warrant at least a year's reflection:

> For the hero, fear is a challenge and a task, because
> only boldness can deliver from fear. And if the risk is
> not taken, the meaning of life is somehow violated,
> and the whole future is condemned to hopeless
> staleness, to a drab grey.

As I pondered these words, anger began to build inside me.

I was angry because I had allowed fear to hold me back for too

many years. I was afraid to take the risk and begin placing one

word behind another. Finally, boldness took over. I didn't care

what people thought. And like the puffins on the edge of Staffa's

high cliffs, I spread my wings and jumped.

Since that time, as Jung's words have continued to

reverberate in my soul, I have said yes to invitations I otherwise

would have refused. A few years ago I said yes to a three-day

speaking engagement in Michigan that terrified me. When I

accepted the invitation, the phone was actually shaking in my

hand. But after much work, it turned out to be one of the most

gratifying experiences of my life. Jung reminds us that without taking risks there can be no real meaning in life. Believing all things prepares the way for boldness.

When you think about your life, much of what you hold dear has been the result of boldness, of believing all things about some venture. The decision to go to college, to graduate school, the decision to marry, to have children, career decisions – all these are fraught with danger. As you reflect on your life, the giant risks that you have taken are most likely your most cherished memories, providing a sense of satisfaction and fulfillment. What matters in life is how you walk through the fire. When destiny calls, don't just stand there. Spread your wings and jump.

Believing All Things When Facing a Bitter Disappointment

Disappointment occurs when an expectation or a hope is defeated or falls short of what had been envisioned. Life often does not work out as we had planned. Without warning, we can experience the loss of a friend, a financial setback or a death in the family. And these intrusions can seem so unfair! They can lead to bitter disappointment.

I know people who were not at worship last week. They will not be in worship next week or in the foreseeable future. Why? They have suffered a serious disappointment – a disappointment with God. They expected God to act in a certain way, and now they feel God has let them down. They have begun to doubt God's goodness and/or fairness.

The ability to believe all things when the storms of life assail you is made possible by a bold way of thinking. This approach is eloquently described by a man named Douglas who was interviewed years ago by Philip Yancey. Douglas was hit by a drunk driver and received a massive blow to the head. After the accident Douglas never knew when a debilitating headache might strike. When this happened, he would become disoriented and forgetful and could not work. Also at this time Douglas' wife suffered a major illness. During the course of the interview, one thing emerged that took Yancey by surprise: Douglas felt no disappointment with God whatsoever. Douglas explained it this way:

The reason is this. I learned first through my wife's illness and then especially the accident, not to confuse God with life. I'm no stoic. I am as upset about what happened to me as anyone could be. I feel free to curse the unfairness of life and to vent all my grief and anger. But I believe God feels the same way about that accident—grieved and angry. I don't blame him for what happened....
We tend to think, 'Life should be fair because God is fair.' But God is not life. And if I confuse God with the physical reality of life—by expecting constant good health, for example—then I set myself up for a crashing disappointment.

Douglas learned to separate life from God. Jesus echoes this in His comment about a tragedy that killed eighteen men in Jerusalem. Jesus said, " Or those eighteen who were killed when the tower of Siloam fell on them – do you think that they were worse offenders than all the others living in Jerusalem? No, I tell you..." (Luke 13:4). Jesus was saying the tower just fell. Call it bad engineering. God did not cause it.

When God is blamed for the misfortunes and losses that are part of life, it can destroy one's faith in God. As a young man, Ted Turner was an avid Christian. He boasted that he had been "saved" seven times and had even considered going into the ministry. However, as an adult, Ted Turner was so opposed to Christianity that when his wife at that time, Jane Fonda, embraced the Christian faith, she was reluctant to tell him and kept it from him for many months. This begs the question: What happened in Ted's life to cause such a dramatic change? For years Ted Turner had watched his younger sister suffer the ravages of lupus. By the time of her death, he had turned from God. His pain and disappointment had taken a heavy toll.

When we see everything as God's *intentional will*, we set ourselves up for a huge disappointment. Leslie Weatherhead in *The Will of God* argues that much of what befalls us can rightfully be considered God's *circumstantial will*. There is a huge difference between God's *causing* something to happen and God's *allowing* something to happen.

My friend and colleague, Rev. Ron Greer, speaks directly to this issue in his excellent book on grief, *Markings on the Windowsill*. Years after a devastating loss and profound disappointment, he was able to affirm from his own experience that "God can *use* what he didn't *choose*." Greer explains, "The Christian faith consistently points to a God who would not cause pain for anyone but who is there to bring growth and new life out of the pain that does come."

We believe all things in the face of a disappointment by not confusing God with the physical realities of life. When bad things happen, we don't blame God. We reach out to God, seeking strength and a sense of the Creator's presence. In this manner over time we *leave a space*, we make room for God to use the loss or disappointment in a redemptive way.

Believing All Things in a Time of Loss

Sooner or later there comes to each of us a season of loss and grief. When that time arrives, *what we believe in our hearts about God –* that harsh or gentle voice that whispers deep inside us that we are loved or condemned – shapes the way we grieve our losses.

I have always believed that faith in a loving God has a positive effect in a person's life. In 2004, Dr. Melissa Kelley, at a national meeting of the American Association of Pastoral Counselors in San Francisco, offered clinical evidence that confirmed my belief. Dr. Kelley presented a major research project that asked one question: Does the way we relate to God influence the way we grieve our losses? Her research strongly indicated that the way we grieve is highly determined by the quality of our relationship with God – prior to the loss. After the seminar, Dr. Kelley told me with excitement that a trusting relationship with a loving God is the most important factor in recovering from a loss.

Her research strongly suggested that a positive, grace-filled relationship with God is statistically a more important factor leading to a favorable grief response than the support of family and friends. This surprised me. In times of grief and loss, people who experience God as gracious, kind and loving, do far better than those who feel in their innermost being that God is judgmental, harsh or capricious. A healthy relationship with God does not take away the pain; it helps us move *through* the pain.

The few individuals in the study who indulged themselves with highly negative thoughts of God actually died before the study was published. These people believed that God had abandoned them, questioned God's love or were convinced that the

Devil was responsible for their losses. Their toxic thoughts, projected onto God, served to alienate them, inhibit their grief response, and compromise their will to live.

People who believe God loves them regardless of the circumstances will ultimately find comfort in times of grief and loss. Others may go their way feeling abandoned or cursed by God. According to Dr. Kelley, a secure relationship with God leads to "personal meaning" and a "positive religious outcome" in the aftermath of a significant loss. If you can believe you are God's beloved son or daughter, especially in times of grief and loss, you are in a much better position to believe God can redeem a difficult circumstance, and ultimately bring meaning from a wrenching loss.

One thing is certain: when you choose your picture of God, you choose your fate. When bad things happen, you can either trust God or blame God. The one-talent man in the parable of the talents chose to blame his master because the servant "knew" his master to be ruthless and unfair (Matthew 25:24). Therefore out of fear he hid his talent and missed the reward. Your everyday experience of God can be a venture of faith or it can be a cynical and bitter existence in which you blame God for the injustices and losses that are a part of life.

Some of those who lost loved ones in the terrorist attacks of 9/11 have had a difficult time dealing with their faith in the midst of their losses. When innocent victims are murdered, people naturally question God's goodness and love. When Guy Barzvi, who worked at the Trade Center, was killed, it caused a crisis of faith for his mother, Gila. The severity of the loss caused her faith to collapse. "I was not a religious person to begin with," she said, "but whatever faith was left to me, I lost when they took my son away."

When the South Tower collapsed, Marion Fontana's husband, a fireman, rushed to Lower Manhattan. When he did not return home, she prayed for days following 9/11 asking God for a miracle. When Marion realized her husband was dead, she stopped praying altogether. She wrote in her memoir, *A Widow's Walk*, that she wanted to believe in God, but she felt like "a spurned friend." For Marion Fontana, God had turned away. And she did likewise.

In contrast, when Travis Boyd's mother died at the Trade Center, his faith in a gracious God helped to hold him together, a faith nurtured over the years at a Baptist church in Harlem. Travis, age 12, raised by a single parent had all the symptoms of grieving a traumatic death. In the midst of a horrific loss, he kept telling himself, "I knew God would get me through it. That's just his way. It allowed me to keep going to school...."

Travis reported he was not angry or bitter. When he accepted the fact that his mother had died, he prayed asking God to take care of him in her absence. Travis Boyd's experience of an enormous loss and the way he relied on a loving God to sustain him are remarkable.

Travis' response to his mother's death is similar to the way the majority of the 200 centenarians studied by Dan Buettner handled their losses. Like Travis Boyd, these older adults reported an unshakable confidence that God was watching over them. Dan Buettner reported that these extraordinary seniors when asked how they were doing, responded, "I feel good, thanks to God." Yet those giving these positive reports were suffering a number of ailments including chronic pain. Buettner said, "They go through life with the peaceful certitude that someone is looking out for them."

When you believe all things about God, that you are loved by God regardless of your circumstances, it not only sustains you in your response to loss, it improves your quality of life. When Jesus said, "I have come that you may have life and have it more abundantly," part of that abundant life is the certainty that God's love does not waver, especially in times of loss and sadness. Our Lord, who was well acquainted with grief, can be a source of real comfort. How you see God in your innermost being –as harsh and distant or kind and gracious – is a decisive factor in how well you will manage a loss.

Love Believes in Your Best Self

In the last century a renowned authority in the field of child development proclaimed that the one thing that is needed to experience a healthy transition from infancy to adulthood is one person who is outrageously crazy about you, someone who believes in your best self. You thrive if you know there is at least one person who loves you no matter how many times you bring disappointment. And after another wrong turn, it is as if you are scooped up in the arms of a love that will not let you go. This kind of love is tenacious and believes in one thing – your best self.

Love chooses to believe, not in your *lesser self*, but in your *best self*. However, because you are not always at your best, you make decisions that are destructive to yourself and others. So it's in your best interest to nourish your best self. But how do you do this?

Years ago I heard the story of a lumberjack that suggests a way to bring out your best. This lumberjack owned a dog that was half collie and half wolf. Even as a puppy, the dog was always growling and biting anyone who dared to come near. The owner gave the dog to a young man who was famous for handling wild dogs. A year later the previous owner returned and could not believe his eyes. This same dog was now friendly, never growled and greeted strangers with interest and a tail that wagged excitedly. The previous owner asked the young man, "What did you do?"

The young man replied, "I fed the collie in him."

In the same way, the challenge is always to nourish your *best* self. To do this, I suggest you learn to respond in a redemptive way when your lesser self ruins someone's day. When this happens, you will need to become fluent in the language of confession. In this language, words like "I was wrong, I apologize," and "Please forgive me," are spoken. The language of confession nourishes your best self because it is the shortest road to forgiveness and reconciliation. In your relationships with friends and family, the language of confession has the power to take you to the land of beginning again. This is essential because before the sun goes down most likely you will have gotten irritated, over-reacted, forgotten something important or in some other way offended someone close to you.

You are going to make mistakes. This is a given. And when you do, you will discover how difficult it is to offer an apology. Instinctively, you will want to justify yourself and lay the blame elsewhere. After all, when you are convinced you are right, there is no need to look inside, reflect, or change yourself in any way. Blaming is easy, but is disastrous to relationships.

A few years ago a couple came to see me for marriage counseling. They described a destructive argument that had erupted between them that quickly escalated to verbal abuse. To me, it sounded as if it happened yesterday. When I asked when this argument took place, she said, "Oh, about three years ago." They had carried the emotional weight of that argument for a long time! A sincere apology most likely would have taken them to a better place. Because they weren't fluent in the language of confession, they drifted into the language of blaming, which only fed their lesser selves.

Years ago I disciplined the wrong child. I wondered why he protested so much. When I discovered what I'd done, I got on my knees, looked my third grader in the eyes and said, "Danny, I've made a terrible mistake. I'm so sorry. I need to help you find a way to forgive me." He placed his little hand on my shoulder and said, "Daddy, this is nothing that a trip to Dunkin' Donuts wouldn't cure." In a flash I grabbed my keys and we were out the door.

While he found a table, I ordered a dozen donuts with drinks. We ate all twelve. And somewhere in the middle of small talk of bicycles, jumping ramps and the Atlanta Braves, forgiveness was given and received. And a father and son believed the best about each other all over again.

Believing the Best in Others

Just as love believes the best concerning you, you are invited to believe the best in others – despite all evidence to the contrary. To do this, you will have to think and act in an extraordinary way. First, you will need to give the offender *the benefit of the doubt.* This means when people mistreat or harm you in some way, you simply say to yourself, "If they could have done it better, they would have." You are saying *on that day* if they could have done it better, they would have. In this way you give them the benefit of the doubt.

Actually, this very thought is found in a rule of baseball. If a base runner touches a base at the same instant the ball is caught by a baseman, the runner is ruled "safe." The runner receives the benefit of the doubt. In the same way, if you receive change from a five dollar bill when you know you gave the clerk a ten, if you assume the mistake was unintentional, you have given that person the benefit of the doubt. You chose to believe in their best self.

Secondly, you will need to offer *a mediating excuse* to those who harm you. When offended or attacked in some way, you look for a circumstance that may have influenced or contributed to your offenders' behavior. In this way, you choose to believe the best in them. In effect, you are saying that apart from a particular circumstance, they would never have harmed you.

Some may protest that this is going too far, that this is outlandish. I totally agree. Love is downright outlandish. When Jesus was nailed to a cross, He prayed to His Father saying: "Father, forgive them; they know not what they do" (Luke 23:34). Jesus gave to those who were crucifying Him the benefit of the doubt *and* a mediating excuse! In effect, He was saying, "If they knew what they were doing, they would not be doing this."

I am astounded that Jesus chose to be gracious to those who were inflicting such agony. If Jesus could do this for those who crucified Him, can we follow in His footsteps? The example of our Lord challenges us to be gracious to those who offend and harm us, saying along with Jesus: "Father, forgive them; they know not what they do" (Luke 23:34). This is "believing all things" at its very best. It is taking the high road that creates a new reality, one conducive to forgiveness and new beginnings.

Believe the Best When Confronting Neurotic Guilt

Loves believes the best in you in the face of bad decisions, mistakes and regrets. However, it has been my personal and clinical experience that when *we* make mistakes, it is easier to be gracious to others than to *ourselves*, whom we hold to a higher standard of accountability. When we miss the mark or fail in some endeavor, we castigate ourselves mercilessly. We question our motives and condemn our character. We indulge ourselves in a barrage of negative self talk that would make a preacher blush. We wallow in a sea of corrosive guilt, endlessly repeating the mantra: "If only I had done it differently!"

Women are particularly vulnerable at this point. They tend to feel responsible for *everything*. Therefore, when things go wrong, they automatically feel guilty. Over the course of their lives, women have accumulated a heavy burden of neurotic guilt. As a matter of fact, Harriet Lerner, a noted author on women's issues, said if you were to show her a woman who was *not guilty*, she would show you *a man!* For women the problem is pandemic.

But more than likely, whether male or female, you know you carry your share of needless guilt. You hear yourself scolding yourself, "I should have done that differently!" You dwell on past mistakes, telling yourself what you should and ought to have done years ago about a multitude of things. And this kind of corrosive thinking only squanders your ability to enjoy life in the present.

Fortunately, there is a way to release this emotional baggage. When you think of those situations when you failed in some way, when you caused heartbreak or needless pain, ask yourself, "Did I do my best *at that time?*" If you are convinced you gave it your best, say these words to yourself very deliberately:

"If I could have done it better, I would have; when I can do it better, I will."

This is a word of grace; it is a gift you give yourself. Over time these words have the power to set you free from neurotic guilt and regret. Whenever you feel that icy hand of guilt begin to squeeze the life out of you because of some misstep yesterday or years ago, start talking to yourself, "If I could have...." After a while you may discover that you are experiencing less neurotic guilt and a lot more joy.

Love believes the best in people and circumstances. But there are times when belief is disappointed. Have you ever believed in someone only to discover later that you've been betrayed? Have you ever believed in a cause that turned out to be a sham? What do you do when you want the best for a family member, but despite your best efforts, that family member continues on a destructive path? What do you do in these situations? Just this: You make the shift from believing in the present to hoping in the future that things will change for the better, not unlike the way God hopes all things for you.

Chapter Two

LOVE HOPES BEYOND ALL REASON

"If you lose hope, somehow you lose the vitality that keeps life moving, you lose that courage to be, that quality that helps you go on in spite of it all."

—Martin Luther King, Jr.

Love Hopes All Things

Love hopes all things. Love can do this because it looks to the future with the expectation that circumstances will improve, even when there is no reason to hope. In short, love looks to the future with faith. The word for hope in the Greek is *elpis*. It is comprised of two words:*"el"* which means "God" and *"pis"* which means "faith." The word literally means faith in God. When we hope, we look to the future with faith in God.

We look to the future with faith in a God who actually *makes covenants with people.* Early in The Book of Genesis we read that Yahweh "cut" an unbreakable covenant with Abraham,

51

the first of many such covenants (Genesis 15:1-20). And a covenant relationship with God changes *everything*. Because of the covenant, we live in the hope that God's promises will be fulfilled in our lives. This transforms the way we live. As children of the covenant, we *live* in hope. We *wait* in hope. In times of sadness we grieve, yes, but not *without hope*. Regardless of our situation, the audacity of hope, empowered by God's covenant, pulls us toward the future.

God, the Promise Giver, the Promise Keeper

Hope must always be underwritten by the promises of God. Otherwise our hope could be dismissed as wishful thinking. However, sometimes the wrong covenant partner makes the promise. When I was a young believer, I had a difficult time living the Christian life. One day while having lunch with a friend, I told him I didn't think I was cut out to be a Christian. I explained that time and again I had promised God that I would live an exemplary life, but week after week, I always broke my promises. It was a time of discouragement and defeat. I was ready to give up the entire endeavor. I will always cherish my friend's wise counsel. He said, "It's not what *you* promise God that counts, *it's what God has promised you*. And as you expect God to keep His promises to you, God does. That's called faith."

Since that day I've endeavored to promise God *nothing*, but by faith to hope for *all things*. In this way I rely on God's power, not mine. The crux of it is to believe that God, the promise giver, will be the promise keeper.

Because love hopes *all things*, I had to learn to keep my hopes *open-ended*, lest I attempted to control God's will for my life. When I hope, I need to be open to *all possibilities*, not just to my own desires and wishes. After all, love hopes *all things*. The most difficult part of this was learning to wait in hope, to hope in *God's time*, not mine.

There was an old adage frequently heard during impromptu theological discussions at Yale Divinity School. It went something like this: "All good theology begins with God." There was wisdom in this saying because in the Judeo-Christian tradition God acts, *then* God's people respond to God's initiative. The action doesn't start with us, but with God. In my early days as a Christian, my theology focused first and foremost on my futile promise-making and resulted in months of frustration. Since that time I have been convinced that any theology not anchored in a covenant relationship with God is doomed to be shallow and woefully lacking.

I was reminded of this many years later when I served as director of a center in Georgia founded to encourage and empower clergy in crisis. We invited pastors from all denominations who had succumbed to the stressors of ministry or who had burned out emotionally and physically to spend a week with us at the center for counseling, support and spiritual direction.

I was impressed with the work ethic and sincerity of these pastors, not to mention their courage and willingness to sacrifice. During our time together I inquired about their faith. I would ask, "What is the centerpiece of your faith in God?" or "Where is the energy in your spiritual life?" or "Tell me what picks you up spiritually when you're discouraged?" Their answers startled me. Most often the pastors' responses sounded like wishful thinking, magical thinking or works-righteousness. They would say things such as, "When difficult times come, I just work harder and pray harder because God helps those who help themselves." When the ministers described the ways they relied on God for courage and direction, one thing stood out: they trusted in *their own strength.*

The personal theology of these pastors was shallow at best and lacked substance. The usual starting point for their theology was a list of the ways they sought to serve or please God. The pastors rarely focused on God as their refuge and strength. This was their undoing. When conflict and adversity came against them or their ministries, they were swept away. Most of them had unwittingly failed to sink their roots deep into a substantive biblical faith – undergirded by the promises of God. For this reason, in times of great stress, they had difficulty looking to the future with hope.

As Christians, we look to the future with hope, remembering God's faithfulness to the covenant promise. This "by faith" remembering actually impacts the present moment which in turn shapes the future. Jürgen Moltmann argues that the very act

of *remembering a promise* is like a benevolent thorn that bores into
"every present moment" and transforms the future. This is
precisely what was missing in the pastors' theology.

In response, I offered every minister a short course in
covenant theology, a theology that recognizes a promise-
fulfillment understanding of scripture. They eagerly received it.
To some of the participants it was an eye-opening experience.
That old adage from Yale was slightly amended. I told them that
all good theology begins with God, *the promise giver, the promise
keeper.* When the ministers began to grasp the concept of resting
in the shadow of God's covenant promise, they seemed to breathe
easier and their spirits lifted.

I longed for these pastors to abound in hope, to see
exemplified in their own lives God's salvation history. I urged
them to keep a record of God's faithfulness to *them.* I instructed
the pastors to write down the stories of God's faithfulness to them
personally and to tell those stories to their children. I reminded
them that this was an integral part of Israel's faith. The exodus
from Egypt was a powerful reminder of God's faithfulness. That is

why this seminal event is always recalled in Jewish celebrations. Just as the memory of God's faithfulness stirred Israel's courage, my hope was that their fresh stories of God's faithfulness could rally their courage as well.

Although this event took place many years ago, I still hear from a few of the pastors from time to time. My prayer is that they will abound in hope as they look to God, the promise giver, the promise keeper.

Like a Thorn That Opens the Future

Hope, like the benevolent thorn that Jürgen Moltmann says pierces every present moment, one day penetrated the emotional flesh of my brother Billy on his last day of school before the summer break. It seemed like an ordinary day, but little did he know that someone had planted in him a vestige of hope that would later shape his life in a surprising way.

Report cards had been given to every student. Billy, a fourth grader, wiped the sweat from his brow and opened the white card in his hand. To his amazement beside every subject was the letter "G," which stood for "Good." His head jerked back in shock. Unbelieving, he asked himself, "I made all Gs?" He looked at the name on the front of the card to make sure there was no mistake. His name was clearly printed there. And he wiped his brow again.

By the time he stepped onto the school bus, he was proud of his report card and himself. Approaching an empty seat, a girl greeted him, "Hi Billy. What did you make on your report card?"

"All Gs," he said nonchalantly.

"All Gs? No, you're kidding."

As Billy handed her the card, he thought to himself, "I've never tried very hard in school. I'm just an average student." Just then his thoughts were interrupted. "Billy," the girl shouted, "You got all Gs! You're a brain!"

Before he could respond, a voice from the back of the bus bellowed, "Billy must be in Mrs. Gibson's fourth grade class. She gives *all* of her students Gs on their last report card."

Billy's euphoric mood was crushed.

But the story doesn't end there. He kept remembering how wonderful it was for someone, especially a girl, to think he was an intelligent person. That fleeting moment of glory touched something deep inside him. He hoped he would have that feeling again. The experience instilled in him the hope of another perfect report card. And that hope was like a seed inside him that had started to grow.

When school began in the fall, he doubled his efforts. So motivated was he to make good grades that once in the seventh grade he got caught cheating. This just made him angry. So he found a way to cheat and *never* be caught: he determined to put *all the answers in his head.* He memorized everything! He found that it took fifteen to eighteen times to work something into his memory.

By the time he reached high school, his memory techniques were perfected. Working hard, he made all A's through four years of a very good high school, except for one B. My brother went on to graduate from Emory University with a major in chemistry and later received an M.B.A. from East Tennessee State University.

Billy's turn-around as a student began with a teacher who, in a symbolic way, "hoped all things" concerning him. And her hope was contagious. For Billy, it was like catching a benevolent disease that spread through his system, ultimately giving him a desire to learn for the sake of learning. When love hopes all things, possibilities for the future are limited only by one's imagination.

A God Who Encourages Hope

In Paul's letter to the Romans he gives a recipe for hope: "For whatever was written in former days was written for our instruction, so that by steadfastness and by the encouragement of scripture we might have hope" (Romans 15:4). God calls us to consider words that were written in former days, that through those *ancient words* we might have hope. For several unforgettable weeks in 1979, through the encouragement of some *ancient words,* God enticed my family to hope as never before.

The years between 1976 and 1979 were the best of times and the worst of times. It was the best of times because we lived in a parsonage on Moon River in Savannah. Our home was part of a beautiful island paradise on deep water. With our little fourteen-foot outboard we explored the intra-coastal water way, the pristine beaches and the islands just offshore. However, after a few years things began to change. The price of gas almost doubled. Because we lived thirteen miles from the church, the sudden increase in the price of fuel caused an increasing financial burden.

When the time came for our oldest son to enter public school, to our dismay we discovered that our five-year-old child would have to board a bus at seven o'clock in the morning, ride forty-five minutes and return home at five o'clock in the afternoon. With three children under the age of five and my working late most nights, my wife, Carole, was growing weary with her long treks from the islands to Savannah's historic district where our church was located. The best of times was fast becoming the worst of times.

We desperately needed to live closer to the church and much nearer to a public school. While praying for guidance concerning whether we should buy a home, Carole was reading in the book of Joshua. That day Joshua's words were not only for the people of Israel, they were for us: "The Lord your God is giving you rest and has granted you this land" (Joshua 1:13 NIV). Carole needed the rest and we needed a home nearer the church. We had arrived in Savannah believing all things. And through the encouragement of scripture, we were learning to hope all things.

After the two of us talked, I was convinced that God was leading us to buy a home. At that time we were the least likely candidates to undertake such a venture. Our savings were meager. However, against all odds we began to look at possible neighborhoods that might meet our needs. While riding through a well-preserved and beautiful section of Savannah, we saw a house for sale with a large side yard that would be perfect for our boys. It was in walking distance to a neighborhood school. What should we do?

Again the words of Joshua prompted us to action: "Three days from now you will cross the Jordan here to go in and take possession of the land the Lord your God is giving you for your own" (Joshua 1:11 NIV). God was moving us down a path we would have never considered. Three days later we signed a contract.

With a strengthening belief that we were headed in the right direction, I met with the trustees of the church who agreed that my housing situation was a huge problem. I left the meeting with their consent to move forward. This was the same group of trustees that a year earlier had declined to purchase a window air conditioner for our parsonage. The God who gives steadfastness and encouragement was prompting us to hope *regardless* of the circumstance.

At this point, all we had to do was raise $10,000 to underwrite the down payment. Twenty percent was required in those days. My annual salary was a little more than the down payment.

In the midst of this, I remembered my father had told me a few years earlier that if I ever needed anything to call him. What is remarkable about this possibility is that my dad and I had been estranged from each other ever since my mother divorced him when I was a small child. He lived in Washington, D. C. and had struggled with alcoholism for many years. I had reconciled with him just a few years prior to our moving to Savannah. Yet Carole and I agreed that our situation warranted a contact. I called and told him we were in the process of buying a house. Before I could say another word, he asked, "Do you need $5,000?"

Shocked, I stammered, "Well….. Yes."

He replied, "I'll send a check tomorrow."

Two days later we received a cashier's check for $5,000. We sold our boat and our two cars for the balance of the down payment. We put aside $3,000 from the proceeds to purchase *two* replacement cars. For a few years we drove a couple of heaps. Nonetheless, signing the papers on our first home was a glorious day in our lives! As children of the covenant—encouraged by scripture to hope—we walked into our own promised land.

The End of the World Will Have to Wait

The opposite of hope is despair, which looks forward to *nothing*. Have you ever lost hope? Have you ever lost *all* hope? I lost all hope one summer as a kid in the fifth grade. A man that I held in high esteem convinced me over a period of several weeks that the world was coming to an end very soon. Combining scripture with world events, he made a very convincing argument.

I learned years later that he was a member of an apocalyptic church that emphasized the imminent return of Christ. Suffice it to say, his words deflated my mood and transformed me from an energetic and venturesome boy into one who suddenly had no future. I was not against our Lord's return, but I *was* looking forward to the sixth grade!

I actually liked school, but when I returned in the fall, I lost all interest in spelling, geography *and* in *The Adventures of Tom Sawyer*. What was the point of it? To make matters worse, these were the early years of the Cold War. In 1953 we were having atomic bomb drills in our classrooms. When my classmates and I heard the siren, we scampered under our desks and sat in a crouched position with our hands and arms covering our heads. The pamphlets that accompanied these drills were filled with images of mushroom clouds, glass flying and flattened buildings.

This was too much for me. I lost interest in everything. To me, it felt like it *was* the end of the world.

As I have reflected upon this experience, I am convinced that I was depressed for several months. I remained that way until December 25th. On Christmas morning I saw a brand new J.C. Higgins three-speed bicycle with my name on it! The end of the world would have to wait. I had new worlds to explore. Before the end of a week, some friends and I had secretly ridden our bikes twenty miles to Forsyth, Georgia. My world wasn't ending. It was expanding! The depression was broken and I returned to school with my usual vigor and curiosity.

However, I have never forgotten those four months of living with a deadening sense of despair. My world without hope had drained the life out of me. But with a little help from Christmas, I was empowered to break the grip of the depression.

In reflecting on my loss of all hope as a fifth grader, I am drawn to an unforgettable scene in the film, *Castaway*. After several years of being stranded on a deserted island, the character played by Tom Hanks assembles a makeshift sailboat from parts of a wrecked plane that have washed ashore over time. After he finally sails off the island and is rescued, he is asked what kept him going when he knew there was no reason to hope. Hanks' character replies, "You keep breathing because you never know what the tide's going to bring in next."

In the same way, with hope we keep placing one foot in front of the other, because in God's providence, we never know what will wash up next on the shores of *our* lives. We never know what God will do next. When Moses led the Israelites across the Red Sea, he had no idea that God would feed the masses with manna from heaven. Like Moses, we keep placing one foot in front of the other because we never know what God will do next. Sometimes we have to hope in the darkness. This is hope at its best.

Someone told me years ago that we need only three things in life to be happy: something to do, someone to love and something to look forward to. When there is nothing to look forward to, life goes flat.

A Vital Hope

There is a particular hope that is essential to life. It is the hope that you will be able to live your life in a meaningful way, where you can relate, create and sing your own song with enthusiasm. And I believe that every now and then in your childhood or youth you leave footprints, traces of who you really are, hints as to the work you're designed to do. For Graham Greene in *The Power and the Glory* these early hints as to your calling in life are never totally absent. "There is always one moment in childhood when the door opens and lets in the future."

When I was in the fifth grade, such a door opened for me when for several months a friend and I published a weekly neighborhood newspaper called *The Penny Press.* We sold it to friends and schoolmates for a penny and were delighted when the readers laughed at our corny jokes and cartoons. Later, as an adult, I was a newspaper columnist for several years, and in one way or another, have been a writer and editor most of my life. Writing has given me my deepest fulfillment, and this calling, like a creative ember, billowed briefly in the fifth grade.

When my oldest son was in the second grade a door opened one morning and we got a glimpse of the future. On that particular Saturday morning he was busy trying to sell a bicycle jumping ramp that consisted of two boards and six bricks. He sat in a chair in front of our house expectantly waiting for someone to respond to a large sign beside him that read: "This Jumping Ramp for Sale - $400." He didn't sell his ramp, but a newspaper man happened to drive by and wrote a column in *The Savannah Morning News* explaining the young man's unique marketing theory: sell something you *don't want* for the price of something you *do want* – like a motorized Go–Cart. This young man later went to business school, earned an M.B.A. from Duke and has been in internet marketing most of his life. The work he was made for, like a compass, kept pointing in the same direction. Marketing has always been his calling, and as a second grader he gave his family a glimpse of it.

Finding and following your calling in life is a sacred quest, one beautifully depicted by Ken Gire in a provocative prayer:

> *Help me, O God,*
> *To listen to what it is that makes my heart glad*
> *And to follow to where it leads.*
> *May joy, not guilt,*
> *Your voice, not the voices of others,*
> *Your will, not my willfulness,*
> *Be the guides that lead me to my vocation.*
> *Help me to unearth the passions of my heart*
> *that lay buried in my youth.*
> *And help me to go over that ground again and again*
> *until I can hold in my hands,*
> *hold and treasure,*
> *Your calling on my life...*

The question that people most often ask is, "How do I find and fulfill the central purpose of my life?" The hope of living a life filled with meaning and passion, the hope of doing the work you love to do – is a hope you *cannot* live without. According to Dr. Lawrence LeShan, the loss of this profound hope is life threatening because it can cause physiological changes on a cellular level.

Dr. LeShan, a research psychologist who for thirty-five years worked with terminally-ill cancer patients, has written convincingly about the power of meaning and purpose and the danger of an unrealized dream. What he discovered was that in many cases as early as eighteen months prior to a diagnosis of cancer, there was a loss of a way of being and relating in life for which the patient could not find a suitable substitute. This loss of meaning, along with a cherished way of relating or expressing one's self in life, served to compromise the patient's immune system. LeShan argues that people experience abnormal cell production every day of their lives, and the body has an efficient way to deal with it. But when stressors accumulate over a long period and become intolerable, the body's "cancer-defense mechanism" is weakened. According to LeShan, the particular stressor that is the most damaging is the loss of hope of living one's life fully.

With no idea of the impact Larry LeShan would have on my life, I first met him in Washington, D. C. following a lecture at Walter Reed Hospital. A few years later in 1985, I invited him to speak in Savannah on behalf of a foundation dedicated to health-related issues. In his lecture he asked his listeners to make a list of those things that might block them from pursuing a life that would give them the most meaning and fulfillment. My list seemed endless. However, because of LeShan's persuasiveness, I vowed to follow my dream *regardless of the cost.*

At that time it would have been much easier for me to settle for security in my professional life than to follow my heart. But I knew such a move would cost me my self-respect, and according to LeShan, possibly much more. Not long after his lecture in Savannah, I accepted a position as a pastoral counselor at the Pastoral Institute in Columbus, Georgia – the most terrifying *and* the most courageous decision of my life.

What LeShan writes and lectures about is a specific despair, a loss of hope that people will ever be able to follow their own dream and be accepted for who they are. Many of the people LeShan worked with had for a period of time denied their true selves for fear they would not be accepted and loved. So they gave into their need for approval from family or friends and denied their true self and to their peril settled for someone else's plan for their lives. LeShan would often remind patients of the poet W.H. Auden's definition of cancer as "a failed creative fire."

This compassionate man never claimed to be a miracle worker. Many of LeShan's patients lived and many died. But now and then he had exceptional patients whose stories have encouraged countless individuals to take bold steps to live as fully as possible. Many of those patients had fulfilling lives, but due to changing circumstances beyond their control, lost a cherished way of being and expressing themselves in life. One of these was named Pedro.

Dr. LeShan met Pedro on rounds. After several visits the doctor asked the young Puerto Rican a question that he asked most his patients: "When were you the happiest in your life?" Pedro responded that he was the happiest when he was the "warlord" of a gang in the South Bronx. When LeShan asked, "What was good about it?" the young man explained that he did not have much of a life living with his mother in a small apartment.

However Pedro's life dramatically improved when he joined the gang. He relished just hanging out with the guys. Having joined the gang at age nine, he quickly came into his own. At age sixteen he became the gang's "warlord," the general when there was a physical conflict with a rival gang. Pedro told LeShan when he was the happiest in his life there were two things good about it: hanging out with the guys and looking out for each other in times of great danger.

But as often happened the gang broke up. Some were arrested, some died on the streets and others were drafted. Pedro found himself ripping off the same old places but he told LeShan there was no joy in it. Pedro was at a dead end. Approximately eighteen months later he was in Sloan Kettering Hospital in New York City with Hodgkin's disease, which in those days was nearly always fatal. LeShan would say that Pedro had lost "his way of being, relating and creating." And for this young Puerto Rican there was no hope of ever replacing his glory days with the gang.

LeShan began the task of searching for a socially acceptable way to restore what Pedro had lost. The doctor decided that a firefighter would meet both criteria: Pedro could live with the guys at the station and when fighting fires, they could look out for one another in times of great danger. When the prospect of becoming a firefighter was suggested, Pedro got excited, and as he prepared for his high school equivalency diploma, his blood work began to improve.

Pedro began to respond positively to the chemotherapy, which had previously been unsuccessful. A few months later he was discharged from the hospital and was seen on an out-patient basis, but he kept up his meetings with LeShan. Pedro had no work history whatsoever, and LeShan helped him write one. A friend of LeShan's gave Pedro a job in a stock room of a small company where he received a letter of recommendation. Then the day came when the radiologist held up an X-ray film and told Pedro it was time to go and take the physical.

Pedro passed it and became a firefighter. That was more than thirty years ago. Pedro married and had several children and from time to time would stop by to see LeShan.

Fifteen years after Pedro first met LeShan, he came to see him with a problem. The firefighter was feeling pressure from his family to take the test for Lieutenant, which he was sure he could pass. But such a promotion would have taken him away from the other firefighters and placed him in an administrative position. Together they decided against his seeking the promotion. They decided not to disturb a life work that had brought healing and was going so well. The hope of singing his song in life with enthusiasm—his living with meaning the life he had chosen—was vital to Pedro's well-being.

It is vital to ours as well.

But there comes to all of us a time when hope *is* exhausted. Such a loss of hope can be heard in the conversation of two men walking the road toward Emmaus. When Jesus, unrecognized, came alongside them, they voiced their despair: "But we had hoped that He was the one to redeem Israel" (Luke 24:21). These men had hoped all things concerning Jesus, only to see their expectations nailed to a cross. For them on that day, hope was not an option.

When you can no longer hope that things will be different, when you come to a point when it only makes sense to stop trying to change things, there comes a time when all you can do is to endure. When love endures all things, it has its own reward – the satisfaction of knowing that your love never faltered, that you stayed the course, that you remained faithful despite the hardships.

Chapter Three

LOVE ENDURES BEYOND ALL EXPECTATION

"When we are no longer able to change a situation—we are challenged to change ourselves."

—Viktor E. Frankl

Love Endures all Things

Love endures all things. This means that love endures with us beyond all expectation. Even when we least deserve it, God's enduring love surrounds us, stands with us, and promises never to forsake us. It may be that God's most extravagant love is the love that endures.

But for us mortals this way of expressing love poses two challenges. First, enduring a situation is difficult for most of us because we are by nature problem solvers. We are action oriented. If we see a picture hanging crooked, we straighten it. If a room is too hot or too cool, we look for a thermostat. It seems we are hardwired for fixing things. And all this conspires against our efforts to endure an uncomfortable situation.

Because our natural instinct is to distance ourselves from a painful experience, the second challenge is not to leave, but to remain present in the situation, not to do something, but to do *nothing*. Love must always remain present because love can never abandon the one loved. To do so would be to cease to love.

When life places you in a situation where you can do nothing, the only way to describe it is unbearable. What do you do when you are helpless to do anything? In life, more often than you would like, you will find yourself wanting to make things better, but you may find there is very little that can be done except to remain present with those who are suffering. But that may be more helpful than you ever imagined.

In the film *The Passion of the Christ* there is an unforgettable scene, where exhausted and weary, Jesus is seen carrying a massive cross. In the background we see His mother watching. She can do nothing but stay close and endure what is happening to her son.

In this scene Mary has asked the disciple John to take her to Jesus. And as she draws near, she hears the horrid sounds of the procession. She stops as if she can go no closer. She hesitates for a moment. Then she remembers a time years earlier when Jesus as a small boy had fallen and scraped His knee on the rocky Judean soil. In her mind's eye, she sees herself running to Him, taking Him in her arms and, with the tenderness of a mother for a child, saying, "I'm here."

Mary runs toward the hideous procession, pushes her way through the crowd and finally reaches Jesus, who has fallen under the weight of the cross. Through her tears she again proclaims her enduring love with the words, "I'm here." Sometimes life is too much to bear. We can't always rush over and make the pain go away for those we love. We can't always help them carry their burdens. Sometimes love means staying near the cross, near those who are suffering.

It means going to the hospital, to a graveside, or to a grieving family, even if you are not sure you can stand the pain. Sometimes, like Mary, we hesitate. There are times when I'm not sure I can open that door and enter that room where pain and suffering have settled in.

But Mary does go to Jesus and later we find her at the foot of the cross. She goes to Him because *love can endure*. It can endure the agony of caring for an aging parent who no longer knows who you are. Love can endure the anguish of dealing with a rebellious teenager or the slow drifting away of an adult son or daughter. When we can no longer make a difference in the lives of those we care about, we express our love with our presence.

Your presence with someone in distress *always* makes a difference. You may wonder how can just being there be of any help? Just this: you make a difference because love builds up (1 Corinthians 8:1). According to Søren Kierkegaard, love builds up by presupposing that love is present in others. When you presuppose love is present in another person, you are built up, and the Kingdom of God is brought near. In the same way that indifference and hatred tear down, love builds up, bringing out the best in you, giving you the courage and strength to endure.

Love's way of building up is eloquently expressed by a friend and colleague who after an accident, has struggled daily with chronic pain. He claims that the love and support of friends who could do nothing for his pain sustained him.

> My anguish has reinforced my conviction that true empathy involves a willingness to embrace each other's suffering while simultaneously knowing that often little can be done to ease the pain. The idea being that 'we can care when we cannot cure' yet knowing our caring is always therapeutic.

When love calls you to stand near the cross, near the suffering, always presuppose that love is present in those who surround you. When you do this, love builds *you* up. And that sustains you in the midst of whatever you must confront.

When Nothing Is All You Can Do

Years ago I found myself in an agonizing situation where all I could do was to endure it. I remember that Little League baseball game like it was yesterday. My youngest son, age nine, was on the worst team in the league. On that sultry summer night both of our pitchers were injured and could not play. The coach asked my son to pitch against one of the better teams.

Michael was a good athlete, but the little guy had never pitched in a Little League game. He would throw a pitch only to watch the ball fly over the fence, wipe the tears from his eyes, and face the next batter. Then throw another pitch, watch the ball fly to center field, see runners rounding the bases, again wipe the tears from his eyes and throw another pitch. He kept at this for seven innings.

I couldn't change anything. All Michael could do as a pitcher and all I could do as a father was to endure it. I prayed that God would somehow redeem this experience in the life of this very young athlete. When the game was over, we celebrated. We celebrated *that the game was over!* Burgers and fries all around.

Actually, I was proud of Michael. He showed at an early age that he could endure a difficult situation. He didn't throw down his glove in a fit of temper and stalk off the mound. He kept pitching, regardless of how badly things were going. This captures the essence of enduring.

There is no greater pain than watching those we love suffer. Feelings of helplessness can sometimes boil over into angry outbursts and destructive behaviors. As long as we can do something to make a difference, the pain is bearable. But sometimes there is nothing we can do. There comes a time when we must step back and do nothing.

Like the waiting father in the parable of the prodigal son, all he could do was scan the horizon. I have the greatest respect for parents who, regardless of their best efforts, have to watch their children suffer the consequences of an addiction to drugs. I have sat and prayed with husbands or wives who have been forsaken by their spouses. They, too, at times must step back and do nothing.

This letting go is eloquently described by Omara, one of the Gulla grandmas who once lived off the coast of South Carolina. She uses some bad theology to make a good point. After a long litany of the troubles she had seen over the course of her long life – of children making destructive decisions leading to drugs and prostitution, she offers a cryptic insight: "Sometimes ya just gotsta leave 'em where the good Lord flung 'em."

Commenting on Omara's words, Michael Downey describes the difficulty of letting go: "But leaving them where the good Lord had put them is her way of expressing a truth we all must learn: often those we care for most deeply are those for whom we can do nothing." Enduring all things is a way of caring deeply for the people we love while at the same time letting go and trusting God with the outcome. Sometimes we have to leave them where "the good Lord flung" them.

Honoring What Matters Most

Several years ago something brushed past me from behind so fast and close that its wind pushed me sideways. A car had missed me by inches. This frightening encounter caused me to begin to reflect on my life. Then another close encounter: a month later I was diagnosed with a malignant melanoma.

Two life-threatening events in the same year plunged me into a season of serious reflection. During this time I was drawn to a large picture window in the second story of my home. Looking down upon a sea of beautiful giant hardwoods, I stood there in wonder and in gratitude, gazing upon a symphony of light and foliage, listening to the treetops rustling in the wind, earnestly thanking God I was alive.

Savoring every sound, I relished the gift of life in the present moment. Then I reached deep inside searching for some vestige of determination to make my life count for something. I visualized the world with me present in it, then saw the world in my mind's eye with me absent. Standing there, switching back and forth between life and death, I was ushered to a new place where I could view my life from a fresh perspective. In this place where priorities become crystal clear, like walking in a cemetery, I pondered my life:

> Am I spending my time on the things that really matter?
> What am I neglecting now that I will regret later?
> How am I treating those I love the most?
> In what ways am I allowing my fears to dictate my life?

These are important questions because if I allow fear or neglect to come between me and the things that really matter in my life, my life won't be worth living. And why should my immune system fight for such a life? *An enduring life honors those things that matter the most to us.*

And now, whenever life is difficult or when I'm fearful, I climb the stairs and stand in front of that window. I let nature's beauty fill my senses. I become aware of the gentle rhythm of the swaying branches. For a brief moment I catch the rhythm and sense a connection. There is something about being in rhythm in a song or a dance that makes you feel a part of it. When I lose myself in the swaying treetops, my thoughts clarify.

Often in life we are out of rhythm. In the novel *A River Runs Through It,* Norman Maclean portrays his father as a Presbyterian minister who "believed that man by nature was a mess and had fallen from an original state of grace... and that only by picking up God's rhythms were we able to regain power and beauty." When we take time to reflect on our lives, we catch a rhythm that connects us to our deepest longings, hopes and dreams. Honoring what is sacred empowers us to endure.

Focus Away from the Pain

There are times for all of us when life becomes very difficult, times when we have no choice but to endure a hardship, a heartbreak, or some form of excruciating pain. At such times our attention is never far from the pain—unless we intentionally shift it elsewhere.

I cannot imagine a worse environment than that of a concentration camp. In that situation, malnutrition, random beatings, disease, and primitive surroundings are part of everyday life. Viktor Frankl, a prisoner at Auschwitz, wrote about his experience and the many ways the prisoners found that helped them to endure. I was impressed by their ability to focus elsewhere even on the agonizing marches that took place in the early morning hours. Frankl often stumbled in the darkness over large stones, and usually with an icy wind in his face.

While marching to his work site one morning, the man next to Frankl whispered, "If our wives could see us now!" This brought thoughts of his own wife to his mind:

And as we stumbled on for miles, slipping on icy spots, supporting each other time and again, dragging one another up and onward, nothing was said, but we both knew: each of us was thinking of his wife. Occasionally I looked at the sky, where the stars were fading and the pink light of the morning was beginning to spread behind a dark bank of clouds. But my mind clung to my wife's image, imagining it with an uncanny acuteness. I heard her answering me, saw her smile, her frank and encouraging look. Real or not, her look was then more luminous than the sun which was beginning to rise.

According to Frankl, the harsh conditions often caused the prisoners to cultivate their inner life to the extent that, at times, they were able to forget their frightful circumstances. The clarity of the images they carried in their minds and their vivid memories could move them to tears. By steadfastly clinging to memories of better times, the prisoners allowed themselves to be transported to another reality, a reality that helped them to endure unbearable days they thought would never end. Sometimes it helps to focus away from the pain.

Love endures, hopes and believes. There is no doubt about this. But we must pause here and ask an important question. If love is so powerful, so life changing, why is it that so few people ever experience it? In John's Gospel we read, "We love, because he first loved us..." (1 John 4:19). But if we look around us, we have to ask why more people aren't experiencing this love. Why aren't more people living a life where love is joyously given and received?

Søren Kierkegaard, in *Works of Love*, answers this way: people miss love because they have been deceived. "To cheat oneself out of love is the most terrible deception; it is an eternal loss for which there is no reparation, either in time or eternity." For Kierkegaard, God's love is the driving force that permeates all creation. And the main reason people fail to experience this love is because they have been misled. In the Adam and Eve story in Genesis, it was *deception* that caused the disruption in the first couple's relationship with God. And variations of this story have been repeated in countless ways ever since. In the next chapter we will expose the subtle ways we deceive ourselves and, in doing so, cause ourselves to miss God's love.

Chapter Four

THREE DANGEROUS DECEPTIONS

"By and large, the gospel of grace is neither proclaimed, understood, nor lived. Too many Christians are living in the house of fear and not in the house of love."

Brennan Manning

Two Brothers Deceived

Scripture is filled with warnings against being deceived and the harsh consequences for those who are. If we take a closer look at the parable of the prodigal son we will see that it actually tells the story of *two* brothers who talk themselves out of their father's love. The terrible consequence of their having been misled is that they separate themselves from their father's love, each in his own way.

The prodigal, who demands his inheritance, leaves his family and goes to a foreign country, does so because he has deceived himself into thinking that happiness and well-being can be found in spending his money on the pleasures of life, far from his father's influence.

However, when the prodigal has spent his money and is starving, when no one will give him anything, he "comes to his senses." In that moment the prodigal knows he has made a terrible mistake. In the midst of a famine, the deception loses its seductive power and frees him to think more clearly. Then he begins the journey back toward his father's love.

The universal appeal of this parable is that the prodigal's story is our story. In the course of a lifetime we journey to many far countries, and like the prodigal, we return home. Each time we discover God's love all over again.

The older brother is also deceived. There are three deceptions that lure the hardworking older brother away from his father's love. Because the deceptions wear a virtuous face, they are subtle, and for that reason they are all the more dangerous.

After years of toil working for his father, doing all the "right" things, the older brother is appalled when his father rejoices at the return of the younger son. I can picture this first-born standing there, arms folded, full of resentment and jealousy.

The older brother will have nothing to do with the banquet saying, "Lo, these many years I have served you and I never disobeyed your command; yet you never gave me a kid that I might make merry with my friends" (Luke 15:29). In response, his father pleads with his older son to join the celebration saying, "It was fitting to make merry and be glad, for this your brother was dead, and is alive; he was lost, and is found" (Luke 15:32).

The older brother fell victim to three dangerous deceptions. First, he lived in close proximity to his father. His father tells him, "Son, you are always with me" (Luke 15:31). However, the older brother's living in *close proximity* to his father was a deception because in reality his heart was far from his father's love. Secondly, the older brother complains to his father that he has always been *obedient.* The older brother is deceived into thinking that his goodness can earn his father's love. Thirdly, there is the deception of *working hard* for his father instead of entering into a grace-filled relationship. He tells his father, "Lo, these many years I have served you..." (Luke 15:31).

These deceptions place a wedge between the older brother and his father and illustrate three areas of danger in our relationship with God:

> the danger of *just being close,*
>> the danger of *just being good,*
>>> the danger of *just working hard.*

The Danger of Just Being Close

There is an old adage that being close only counts when throwing darts or playing horse shoes. This saying points to the all-important distinction between being on target and just being close. Similarly, in our relationships with each other there is an enormous difference between occasionally being together and sharing an intimate relationship. I am using the word "close" in the sense of close proximity, of being in the same space. I am not referring to a close relationship where two people know and trust each other deeply. My use of this term refers exclusively to a close physical proximity.

For instance, several years ago at a social gathering, a man that I barely recognized referred to me as a "good friend." I was shocked because I hardly knew him. Frankly, I didn't know much about his personal life or his family. Through civic, church and professional obligations, we saw each other frequently; but we seldom spoke to each other. We were just two men who from time to time happened to share the same space. I knew nothing of his hopes and dreams. He knew nothing of my pain and sadness. In short, there was no friendship. Just occasional closeness.

Someone has described intimacy as an experience of "into-me-see," where we allow someone to see below the surface of our lives revealing who we are. This is the hallmark of true friendship. The man who referred to me as a "good friend" had confused an acquaintance with a friendship. In our relations with one another this may lead to disappointment; but if we allow this to happen in our relationship with God, it can be perilous.

One day as Jesus was teaching and journeying toward Jerusalem, He spoke directly to the all-important distinction between occasional togetherness and an intimate relationship. He

was asked, "Lord, will those who are saved be few" (Luke 13:23)?
In response, Jesus said that many would seek to enter the narrow
gate, but would not be able. Jesus then offered a parable of a
householder who had gone to bed and locked his door. When
asked to open the door, he refused telling the people outside, "I do
not know where you come from" (Luke 13:25).

In response, those outside attempted to persuade the
householder, (who is Jesus himself) to open the door by saying,
"We ate and drank in your presence and you taught in our streets"
(v.26). Those rejected were shocked to discover that they were so
close (in proximity), yet so far away in terms of a relationship.

When Jesus said, "I do not know where you come from,"
He was referring to the ancient Jewish custom of always knowing
where someone is from prior to pursuing a friendship. When Jews
first met, the first thing disclosed was where they were from. They
disclosed their tribal and family names. But those locked outside
only had a passing acquaintance with the Lord. There was no
relationship, just occasional closeness.

In this passage, Jesus sounds a warning to those who frequently attend church, Sunday School and Wednesday night suppers. When they stand before the Lord, it will be a tragedy if all they can say is, "Lord, we ate and drank in your fellowship hall. Your message was taught in our church." Such statements would confirm that they had not moved beyond occasional closeness. Just being in close proximity to a Christian community is dangerous because it can lull us into *the illusion* of a relationship with Christ!

Ministers and priests are particularly vulnerable to this deception because we stand close to the things of God – the scriptures, the altar, the sacraments. Because we as clergy can become so absorbed in our ministry, our relationship with God can easily lose its priority. This deception is beautifully portrayed in the cartoon "Family Circus." A little girl is pictured sitting in church with her mother, and she asks her mom, "Is our pastor a friend of God's or do they just know one another through business?"

Because it is our business to be close to things of God, our first priority should be to let our roots grow deep into the soil of God's marvelous love. Otherwise, we may confuse our closeness to things sacred with an intimate relationship with a Lord who called His disciples "friends."

One person that Jesus called "friend" was Peter. Yet after Peter denies Christ, the next time they meet face to face, Jesus does not ask Peter about his faithfulness or his loyalty. Jesus simply asks him, "Peter, do you love me?" Jesus questioned the depth of Peter's relationship with Him. Love was the standard. That is why "just being close" is counterfeit.

When we consistently invite God to see beneath the surface of our lives, revealing where we come from – our brokenness, our guilt, our pain and suffering, as well as our joys and celebrations – we bring to God our *real selves*. In this way, we are better able to hear God's voice and respond.

A vibrant relationship with God can be supplanted by just being close, but the comfort of closeness is enough to keep us at it for years. Similarly, a focus on "just being good" can do the same thing. Who would ever find fault with our being good and obedient? Hardly anyone. And that's the problem.

The Danger of Just Being Good

I always wanted to be good, but not *too good*. As a teenager, for me the market value of being good hit rock bottom simply by watching westerns. In movies I saw goodness depicted as weakness countless times:

> A small town waits in fear because the people have been warned that a gang of hardened outlaws are headed their way. The good townsfolk are no match for the bad guys, who are armed to the teeth. The sheriff and the preacher are among the inept, who lock themselves in the jail for their own protection. The only hope for the good citizens is a desperado who happens to be passing through. Looking into the eyes of a trusting lad, something noble stirs deep within the wrinkled drifter. Just in the nick of time, the gunslinger inspires the townsfolk and with guns blazing saves the day!

Watching this theme played out repeatedly, the logic was inescapable: *bad is strong; good is weak.* As an adolescent, I felt the need to court danger in order to assert my manhood. I chose not to be identified with the insipid church folk portrayed in the westerns.

The same year I was elected president of the Methodist Youth Fellowship I found myself in a sheriff's office at 3:30 in the morning, calling someone to take me home. I wanted to be good, but not *too good* lest I be identified with those people whom Mark Twain spoke of as being "good in the worst sense of the word."

No one group embodies the danger of "just being good" better than the Pharisees. The driving force of their lives was keeping the law. This group with their tenacity for obedience to the law drew the sharpest rebukes from Jesus:

"Alas for you, lawyers and Pharisees, hypocrites! You cleanse the outside of the cup and dish, which you have filled inside by robbery and self-indulgence" (Matthew 23:25 NEB)! The Pharisees' problem, basically, was the deception that *doing* something guaranteed the quality of *being* what God expected. Therefore, the harder they worked at it, the more entitled they felt they were to think of themselves as better than others.

The Pharisee described in Jesus' parable of the publican and the Pharisee is scripture's prime example of being good for all the wrong reasons. The parable was told in the presence of a group of Pharisees, so confident in their own goodness, they looked down on everyone else. In this parable the Pharisee looks around at a group of adulterers, thieves and at a lonely tax collector at his side and prays, "God, I thank thee that I am not like other men, extortioners, unjust, adulterers or even like this tax collector" (Luke 18:9-14). Those who become caught up in a radical obedience to the law are vulnerable to pride and arrogance.

The legalists of today, those who worship at the altar of keeping rules and living a totally pure life, remind me of the Pharisees of yesterday. A few years ago I was shocked to read that Orthodox Jews in Israel were making women move to the back of the bus so that conservative Jews would not look upon the women and lust. There were several clashes with the women because a few of them had refused to move, one of whom was hospitalized with injuries.

These incidents remind me of an ancient group of pious men known as the "bruised and bleeding Pharisees" who, in order to keep from sinning, would close their eyes whenever they saw a woman. They were named the "bruised and bleeding Pharisees" because they kept colliding with walls and obstacles! The Orthodox Jews on the buses could take a lesson from their bruised forebears.

Parable of the Chocolate Shop

The hypocrisy of those who pride themselves in being pious is portrayed in the film *Chocolat*. This delightful and whimsical fable, that unfolds much like a parable, tells the story of what can happen when keeping the law collides head on with grace and love. This film exposes the thin façade of "just being good" and how it can be used to conceal the lust for power and the need to control.

In a small town in rural France, life was orderly, pious and tranquil. It was kept that way by the town's mayor, a modern-day Pharisee. Vianne Rocher and her daughter arrive in town during the time of Lent and establish a small chocolate shop. This raises the ire of the mayor, who vows to rid his town of the two intruders and their chocolate delights.

But the chocolate shop becomes a place of healing and reconciliation. Vianne's kindness, good humor, and delectable chocolates soon win her customers despite the mayor's efforts to shut her down. Slowly her shop becomes a shelter for people burdened with brokenness – within themselves and with each other. What customers experience in the shop is a taste of pure, unadulterated grace.

With Vianne's encouragement, one of her customers finds the strength to leave her abusive husband and finds sanctuary with Vianne and her daughter. There she is offered not only shelter and friendship but a new lease on life. Another customer, long estranged from her daughter and grandson, warms to Vianne and her hot chocolate and begins to repair the relationship with her grandson right there in the shop. While Vianne is selling chocolate, she offers compassion and grace free of charge.

As Vianne and her new friends are celebrating the goodness of God's grace and mercy, the mayor fasts excessively and declares open war on Vianne and all outsiders who refuse to conform. The mayor is convinced that his acts of self-denial guarantee a quality of being before God. The outside of his cup looks clean, but inside he is full of pride and arrogance. The mayor even *dictates* what the young priest will preach on Sundays – a diatribe on keeping the law and making their town safe from outsiders. The mayor does this while deceiving the townsfolk about his own broken marriage.

But in the end, even the mayor falls under the spell of the chocolate. On the evening before Easter Sunday, in a fit of righteous indignation, he breaks into Vianne's shop to destroy her sinful creations. As he is slashing at a chocolate figurine in the display window, a piece of chocolate touches his lips. The taste of the chocolate causes the mayor's pent up yearnings to explode in an eating frenzy. Hand over fist, he crams the chocolates into his mouth. He climbs into the display window and gorges himself until he passes out.

Early Easter morning, he is awakened by Vianne who offers him a remedy for his self-inflicted condition. After taking a sip, the disheveled mayor looks at her as if to say, "What now?"

And she, the outcast, offers him a taste of pure grace when she says, "No one will ever know." Vianne extends grace even to her adversary. When the mayor's crusade against Vianne is exposed for the hypocrisy that it truly is, he surrenders. And in doing so, he exchanges his pride for a healthy dose of humility.

This parable exposes the shadow side of just being good. In stark contrast to love and grace, the self-righteousness of the mayor acts as a thin veil that conceals his need to control, accuse and condemn. Frankly, there is nothing redemptive in just being good. Healing and reconciliation flourish, not at the village church, but at the chocolate shop! When we allow ourselves to be caught up in just being good to the exclusion of love, it's an invitation to pride and arrogance, and these two demons have a way of renouncing love in favor of power.

Alongside the deception of just being good is the deception of working hard. Just as obedience and good behavior can be thought of as a relationship, the same can be said for rushing headlong from one good work to another. However, because of our Protestant work ethic, working hard may not appear to be a

threat to one's spiritual life. Hence, the danger.

The Danger of Just Working Hard

While walking down the main street in Providence Town on Cape

Cod, I saw a T-shirt walking toward me with the following

message:

Jesus is Coming Soon.
Look Busy!

I laughed out loud. The admonition to look busy at the

return of Christ is ludicrous. But I found these words humorous

and thought provoking. The suggestion that simply looking busy

would please the returning Lord strikes a chord because our culture

places such an emphasis on working hard or at least looking like

you're working hard.

When I greet people whom I've not seen for a while, often

they will ask, "Are you staying busy?" Although it's a ridiculous

question, it points to a cultural obsession. The reason the message

on the T-shirt is funny is that it's so true. The reality is that many

Christians will immerse themselves in relentless activities *for* God to the neglect of ever entering a vital relationship *with* God. Why? Because a relationship is far more demanding.

Even on a human level, we would sometimes rather do things for people than relate to them. In my counseling practice with couples, frequently I am presented with the following scenario:

Wife: "George, you hardly ever talk with me anymore. You never share your feelings. We're married, but I wonder if I really know you. Sometimes I wonder if you really love me."

Husband: "Marge, you know my work is demanding – I can't believe you doubt my love. Why do you suppose I work so hard? It's for you and the kids."

Wife: "Honey, you are a wonderful provider. It's just that I don't know who you are these days."

Husband: "I am the same guy that promised to take care of you years ago, and that's what I've done. I tell you I love you. I treat you decently. What else do you want?"

Wife: (with tears brimming) "I want a relationship."

For this husband, working hard was his way of showing his wife that he loved her. He's working hard; but she's not getting the message. Where could he have gotten such an idea? In America, it is in the air we breathe. Our Protestant work ethic is woven into the very fabric of our lives.

For whatever reason, for most of my life I have felt that I needed to work hard to be accepted and loved. This is what I have been taught in various ways across the years. As long as I did what my parents, my peer group, my professors and my parishioners wanted, I was accepted and rewarded. In these relationships, the harder I worked, the more secure I felt.

It was second nature for me to transfer this graceless way of relating to people to my relationship with God. Like the husband in my counseling office, I was tempted to proclaim to God, "Look how hard I've been working! How can my devotion be doubted?" This kind of thinking kept me in bondage for years. In those days I had an idealized picture of all the things I should be doing and a long list of things I had promised God I would do, yet had failed to do. When I prayed, I could not see the face of a gracious God. All I could see was my long list of shortcomings. So what did I do? Sadly, I rolled up my sleeves and worked harder.

When Working Hard Is the Total Focus

Working hard to earn God's love is one of the subjects Jesus addresses in the Sermon on the Mount. Jesus paints a picture of an active and vibrant relationship with God that includes our deepest needs as well as our struggles with anger, fear, lust and forgiveness. As we bring these real-life issues into the presence of God and wrestle with them, our relationship deepens. With these and other concerns, we are instructed to pray to the Father who desires to give "good things to those who ask him" (Matthew 7:11). But when working hard *for* God takes the place of interacting *with* God, we don't find ourselves asking God for much of anything. Like the older brother – we are too busy with the things at hand.

To make the issue perfectly clear, Jesus offers a stark contrast between cultivating a relationship with Him and working hard in His name. Our Lord's warning is strong because this deception is as prevalent as it is dangerous:

> "Not everyone who says to me, 'Lord, Lord,' shall enter the kingdom of heaven; but he who does the will of my Father, who is in heaven. On that day many will say to me, 'Lord, did we not prophecy in your name, and cast out demons in your name, and do many mighty works in your name?' And then I will declare to them, 'I never knew you; depart from me, you evil doers (Matthew 7:21-23).'"

When working hard takes the place of knowing God, the work becomes contaminated. It is a form of idolatry. In this passage, it is the hardworking follower of Christ who is seen as an "evil doer." These are strong words because the deception is so compelling. It is only when we come to know God first hand that we discover the tenderness of God's love. But most people will never experience the tenderness of God's love because they've been deceived into thinking that they haven't worked hard enough.

In addition to just being close, just being good and working hard to earn God's approval, there are other hidden dangers that can stand between us and a satisfying relationship with God. When it comes to beholding God, our fearful projections can cloud the picture. In the next chapter we will explore some ways to see God with more clarity.

Chapter Five

GOD'S PORTRAIT DAMAGED AND REDEEMED

"For now we see through a glass darkly, but then face to face."
The Apostle Paul

Creating God in Your Own Image

Deep inside every person there is an internal picture of God. This mental image can be that of a gracious and loving God or it can be harsh and vengeful. People are usually surprised to discover that this image is formed by the time a child is three years of age. All children speak of God, and their primitive pictures and impressions of God can leave an indelible impression that has the power to influence one's thoughts of God for years to come. But where do these earliest images of God come from?

David Heller, a research psychologist, claims that all children are "young theologians" who have very definite ideas about God, often viewing God in a negative light. Heller's research challenges the myth that children see God as an idealized grandfather figure. "All the children I studied seemed to weave their most pressing emotional concerns into the fabric of their God creations...." Whatever issues that dominated family life, such as rejection, neglect, criticism or control, seem to make their way into the child's view of God.

The way a parent holds, cuddles, makes eye contact and speaks to an infant serves to paint an internal picture of how the child is regarded. Later, when the child speaks about God, the child will call forth his or her internalized parental images. In this way all children are theologians, but their theology is derived from their closest encounters, the God-like figures of their imperfect parents. For this reason, the pictures of God that were crafted as children haunt us as adults.

An example of how a projection from childhood affects one later in life was demonstrated in a therapy session conducted by Dr. Larry Stephens, a counselor at the Minirth-Meier Clinic in Dallas, Texas. His client was an adolescent named Brent:

Brent sat in my office and described his father as unemotional, undemonstrative and distant. 'My dad never had much to say to me,' he told me, 'unless he got really mad.'

Later in our conversation, I asked Brent to describe how he pictured God. 'I see God,' he said, 'as an old man sitting on the porch. He doesn't do anything. He doesn't say anything – unless you do something wrong and make him mad.'

'Do you notice,' I asked him, 'how much your description of God sounds like your description of your dad?' He seemed startled and opened his mouth to object. Then he said, 'You know, I think you're right.'

Like Brent, people are usually surprised when they discover that the face of God looks very much like the face of a parent. Once in a therapy session, a charming elderly client who wore a black patch over her left eye stated that she had not been to her Catholic church for several weeks and felt "unshriven." When I asked what that meant, she said she felt guilty and needed confession and absolution. After a long silence I asked, "I wonder what God's thoughts are of you today?" She laughed, shook her head and blurted, "Oh, don't ask!"

"Why not?" I inquired.

"Because I feel God has turned away from me."

"Has that ever happened before in any other relationship?"

"Yes, my mother. She was not very assertive. When I went to the hospital after the automobile accident, only my father came to be with me. You know, when I was nine and lost my eye."

As a nine-year-old, the one time in her life when this woman desperately needed the warmth and comfort of her mother, her mother was absent. It felt as if her mom had turned away. Now, as a ninety-year-old woman, it seemed like God had returned the favor. My client's relationship with her mother shaped the way she felt about God – more than 80 years after her tragic loss.

Toward the end of our session, this lovely woman said she would be interested in knowing something of God's thoughts of her. She wondered what they might be. In response, I shared from scripture some thoughts God might have concerning her. She was pleasantly surprised that the thoughts were all positive and affirming of who she was – a person who mattered to God, greatly beloved and highly favored, *regardless* of her absence at Sunday worship.

Her immediate response was, "I *never* would have thought that. I hope it's true." Moments later, as she was preparing to leave, as I often do, I asked how she felt. Smiling broadly, and with a triumphant wave of her hand she proclaimed, *"I feel great. I feel shriven!"*

The primitive pictures of God that we paint as children stay with us as adults. If our parents were harsh, God will be seen as harsh. If our parents were distant, God will be seen as distant and uncaring. Hopefully, as we mature as Christians, we will learn to see God in a more positive light. But for this to happen we must become aware of what our feelings are toward God.

Recovering from a Distorted Picture of God

More often than we would suspect the beautiful contours of God's love and kindness, His grace and favor become distorted and twisted into a distant and disappointed God. I know this was my experience and the experience of a large number of the people I either interviewed or counseled. For most of my life's journey I was held in bondage to a harsh and demanding God of my own making. Had I been asked to describe my thoughts of God, I would have answered, "God is disappointed in me *again*."

Out of curiosity for the past fifteen years I have asked hundreds of people, "What are God's thoughts of you today?" After a few years, their responses became very predictable. Most often people said something like: "Well, I haven't been reading my Bible as I should. I haven't been praying very much. And I've been neglecting church." What I heard and continue to hear can be summarized in one sentence: "I guess I just don't measure up."

For most people, approximately eighty-seven per cent of those I have interviewed, the prevailing attitude was that they have been weighed in the balances and have been found deficient. Because they feel this way, God's love is not deserved and for this reason God remains distant. In various ways, people from all walks of life have told me they have not been diligent enough in their perfectionist efforts to please God.

Also, several prominent Christian writers attest that they, too, have struggled with a negative picture of God, one that kept them at a distance from God's love. Philip Yancey, the former editor of *Christianity Today* and a prolific writer, as a young man pictured God as judgmental. Even as a youngster, he could not miss the double message sent by his church. "Although I heard 'God is love,' the image I got from sermons more resembled an angry and vengeful tyrant." He pictured "a God who forgives but reluctantly, after making the penitent squirm. I imagined God a distant thundering figure who preferred fear and respect to love...." Yancey described himself as "resentful, wound tight with anger, a single hardened link in a long chain of ungrace learned from family and church."

In God's providence, Yancey's writing career placed him in a collegial relationship with Dr. Paul Brand, a medical doctor renowned for his work with leprosy patients. Yancey's relationship with Dr. Brand provided a steady stream of cool water for Yancey's thirsty and sometimes cynical soul. Under the influence of Dr. Brand, Yancey's ideas of a vengeful God were discarded over time. In their place he nurtured a new picture of God, a loving, gracious and compassionate God that Yancey writes about extensively in his book *What's So Amazing About Grace?* What made the difference for Philip Yancey was the study of scripture and a redemptive relationship with an extraordinary individual. Yancey says of Dr. Brand, "From people such as him, I learned grace by being graced."

Whenever I read one of Yancey's books, I have the feeling I am walking with a fellow traveler. Both of us are like recovering legalists. Likewise, our image of a demanding God was challenged by someone whose life and witness pointed toward a more gracious God. And for both of us the process has taken decades.

Sometimes an unfavorable picture of God is reinforced by what is heard in church. As a little girl, Dr. Roberta Bondi, a professor at Candler School of Theology, heard almost every Sunday that she was a sinner. All she had to do was to believe that God loved her and she would be saved. In *Memories of God* she admits that she could not believe it. She asked herself, "How could God love me in spite of my sins if they were bad enough to make God's own Son die?" She figured God was like her earthly father except worse. Furthermore, the pictures of God portrayed in the church only reinforced her distorted image of God – as authoritarian, perfectionistic and exploitative. Such thoughts of God caused this precocious girl and later articulate woman to feel totally unworthy, inadequate and depressed.

Dr. Bondi's new way of seeing God would come from a most unlikely place. While studying at Oxford, she stumbled upon the writings of the first great Christian monks of the Egyptian desert. From them she would learn that God is very different from the God she had known. The desert monks wrote of a God, "who is much more willing than human beings to make allowances for sin, because God alone understands our circumstances, the depths of our temptations, the extent of our sufferings." For the monks, God was less interested in sin and more interested in the sinner. But more importantly, God as portrayed by the monks expected less of her than her earthly father! God was primarily interested in her well-being, not her performance. She discovered she did not have to work harder.

For Dr. Bondi the emerging picture of a gracious God painted by the desert monks was a breath of fresh air. She was on her way to recovery, and in the process, discovered a God who "actually liked us!" As you read her story, you can feel her excitement as she allowed the emerging picture of a gentler God lift her mood, boost her self-confidence, and put a huge skip in her step. But most people don't recover from a damaged picture of God. They limp along unaware of the flawed portrait of God they've unwittingly painted deep within themselves.

When the late David Seamands, a longtime professor at Asbury Theological Seminary, would ask students about God, their answers were often contradictory. After counseling hundreds of students, probing deeply into their spiritual lives, Dr. Seamands discovered a conflict between what genuine Christians *thought* about God and what they *felt* about God. His students would talk about a God of love and grace, but on a feeling level would describe God as harsh and demanding. After one of his counselees had given Seamands his glowing thoughts on God's love, Dr. Seamands asked the student what his "felt sense" was of God. The student answered: "I don't think He [God] really cares for me; I'm not sure He knows I exist. If He does, I'm not sure He's concerned." What the students *felt* about God was in stark contrast to their *thoughts* about God. Regrettably, the students agreed that their negative feelings about God (in their inner being) are what actually shaped their spiritual life.

Dr. Seamands was convinced that the most determinative factor in a person's spiritual life was what he called "a felt sense of who God is and what He is really like." I am persuaded that for most people this "felt sense" of what God is like has been corrupted. Because this damaged sense of God's nature is hidden in our feelings, it is seldom brought to the surface and healed. And this self-deception saps the spiritual vitality of a great number of earnest and committed Christians. When this happens, the tragedy is that we settle for less than what God intends for us.

The way you see God creates a palette from which you paint a self-portrait depicting how God sees you. If you see God in harsh and judgmental tones, you will likely see yourself in God's eyes as condemned. Conversely, if you see God in colors that are kind and gracious, you will likely see yourself in God's eyes as forgiven and loved.

Retouching a Worn-Out Picture of God

Whatever is in your heart has a way of finding its expression in your life. Were you to paint a picture of God, what mood would be expressed? What colors would fill your canvas? Would your picture be bright and cheerful or dark and foreboding? Would the picture be alive and active or dull and boring?

Years ago I asked a group of therapists to paint their picture of God. After handing out magic markers and paper, I instructed them to draw and color a picture of God and to include themselves in the picture. The experience turned out to be more revealing than I could have imagined. One person drew herself as a stick figure crouching in the lower corner of her paper with a look of utter bewilderment. The rest of the paper was blank. She declined to comment on her picture. The majority of the pictures portrayed a stately God with His humble servant. The colors were muted; the action stilted. The dull colors and the lack of action suggested a spiritual life that could only be described as dreary.

However, one picture stood out from all the rest. Awash in color and sweeping action, the picture was a thing of splendor. The therapist had painted himself dancing in the palm of God's hand. Surrounded by vibrant hues of yellow, orange and red, God was depicted as delighting in the dancer. The mood was celebratory. My colleague's picture was an epiphany of sorts. I should not have been surprised by my friend's glorious picture. His life, his encouraging spirit, the way he honored people, the attention he paid to matters of faith were all natural outpourings of a remarkable internalized picture of God and his joyful response to that God.

Deep in our heart is an image of God. We have already chosen the colors and have painted the picture. If we've painted God as harsh and judgmental, it should not surprise us that despite our best efforts, we feel we don't quite measure up. Conversely, if we paint God in vibrant colors – as a waiting father who delights in us – there's a good chance we'll experience God as gracious and loving.

The good news is you can begin to re-touch your picture of God whenever you choose. But be patient; it takes time. When the Apostle Paul said you should be transformed by the renewing of your mind, he did not indicate the change would take place immediately (Romans 12:2).

It takes time to work new thoughts and ideas into your soul. I believe this is what George McDonald had in mind when he said: "As the world must be redeemed in a few men to begin with, so the soul is redeemed in a few of its thoughts, and works, and ways to begin with: it takes a long time to finish the new creation of this redemption."

For those who are interested in making some changes in the way they see God, George McDonald shows us where to begin. As with any artist, it is seldom a bold stroke. It consists of tiny brush strokes here and there, choosing our colors carefully. The colors on our canvas, of course, represent our thoughts of God. It's in our thinking about God that makes us miserable or joyful, can help us in a crisis, or throw us into despair. It's all in our thinking. And according to McDonald, redemption does not come in huge sweeping changes in the way we think. For him "the soul is redeemed in a few of its thoughts...."

When God reveals himself to us, it is through a few fresh thoughts here and there, like small brush strokes. For me, God was always revealed a thought at a time. The idea that God would take care of me was the predominant thought that sustained me during my childhood years. In college, I discovered God as a loving Father who cared enough to come looking for me. In my young adult years, I was captivated by the thought that God is loving and kind beyond all expectation. And more recently the thought that "I am God's beloved" continues to work itself into my soul. A few thoughts lodged in my heart have made all the difference. But there would not have been a faith journey had God not made me *aware* of my negative thoughts and feelings toward God. This awareness is what set me on my journey.

Frederick Buechner has said that all theology is autobiography. With this in mind, the next chapter will present God's love on the canvas of personal experience. God's love is not an abstraction. What we know about God comes to us in the form of a narrative – in *the stories* of creation, *the stories* of Moses and David in the Old Testament and *in the stories* of Jesus and Paul in the New Testament. A picture of God's love is gleaned from these stories and, believe it or not, from *our stories* as well. And if we look closely at these personal narratives, they will reveal in surprising ways God's relentless love.

Chapter Six

LOVE'S GIFT RESTORED BY GRACE

"What would it mean, I ask myself, if I too came to the place where I saw my primary identity in life as 'the one Jesus loves'? How differently would I view myself at the end of a day?"
—*Philip Yancey*

God Experienced As Loving and Kind

My early years as a Christian were tumultuous with many ups and downs. It was not until I was a young man in my late twenties that I began to experience God with some consistency. It began with a summer on the Jersey coast.

A year after graduating from seminary, I spent a sensational summer on the beaches of Ocean City, New Jersey, working with college students in a ministry with Campus Crusade for Christ. One morning I grabbed some books, walked to the beach and stretched out. Presently, Marilyn Henderson, a friend and colleague whose ministry and faith I respected and envied, joined me on the beach. I was reading a book legions of men would call sacred – *Sports Illustrated*. Marilyn, on the other hand, had brought her Bible and some devotional material.

After a while, without a trace of judgment in her voice, she turned to me and said, "Buddy, you probably would spend more time with God if you knew the God you were spending time with. I'm not sure *your* God is worth the effort."

I did not protest. Her words were not a condemnation; they were an invitation.

There was something compelling and attractive about Marilyn's relationship with God. It gave her radiance and drew her to seek God in ways I could not comprehend. I knew God loved and cared for me, but Marilyn knew God in the depths of her being! It was as if she delighted in God, and God delighted in her. I wanted what she had, and that summer she showed me a way to get started.

Marilyn handed me her Bible and suggested that I look at Psalms 147:11. The passage reads as follows: "God's joy is in those who reverence Him, those who expect Him to be loving and kind" (Psalms 147:11,TLB). She asked, "Why do you suppose it gives God joy when we expect God to be loving and kind?"

"I suppose, because most people don't expect God to be loving and kind to them personally," I said. "They expect less." I knew I did.

Marilyn then challenged me to begin to look for God's kindness in my everyday experience. She suggested that every time I witnessed God's kindness in my life or someone else's life that I offer a simple prayer, "Thank you, God. You are loving and kind." Her challenge intrigued me. I yearned to experience God in a more personal way. So I began to keep my eyes open, looking for a chance to catch God in an act of kindness.

The next day I was to drive some students to Philadelphia. We were almost out of town when one of my riders realized he had left his sleeping bag in the lobby of the hotel. As I turned the car around, I was a little irritated. However, once back at the hotel, a distraught student ran toward my car.

"I can't believe you're back here! I tried to flag you down as you were driving off," she blurted.

And wiping the tears from her eyes, she explained that just moments before our departure, her mother had called to tell her that she was on her way to the University of Pennsylvania Hospital for emergency surgery. Now suddenly the ride she desperately needed was back at the hotel. Some would call it a coincidence; I chose to call it God's kindness.

While driving to Philadelphia, I reflected on Marilyn's challenge. In the silence, I prayed, "Thank you, God. You *are* loving and kind." God's immense love flooded my heart. I was amazed that I would be provided such a blatant example of God's kindness. One thing was certain: God had used the carelessness of one student to answer the urgent prayers of another. And, in the process, I was given an unforgettable portrait of God's kindness.

I will be forever grateful to Marilyn for helping me discover God's love and kindness firsthand. This prompted me to help others do the same. Years later this remarkable woman married Denny Rydberg, the President of Young Life.

Whenever I speak or write emphasizing that God is primarily loving and gracious, it often draws a mild protest.

People argue: "The Bible says we should *fear* God." And they are correct. There is an aspect of God that is holy and righteous, the Lord God Almighty, which makes God unapproachable. Annie Dillard had this in mind when she said that the liturgy of the high church is the way people have learned to talk to God without being blasted to pieces. This notion that God is not safe is evidenced by Isaiah, who when given a vision of God, falls on his face in terror (Isaiah 6:1-7). From what people have told me, this is close to the picture that many folks have of God.

Luke   gives us a glimpse of *both* sides of God's nature when he describes the early church as walking in the fear of God and in the comfort of the Holy Spirit (Acts 9:31). The majority of people that I've encountered are well aquainted with *the fear of God* but know little of *the comfort of God*. Their picture is one-sided. The stark and formal images of God often obscure a more intimate God that Jesus referred to as "Abba," that is best translated "Papa." Much of my life has been an attempt to correct this one-sided, and hence, distorted picture of God.

Living as God's Beloved

For most of my Christian life something kept me from claiming God's love in all its fullness. Something hidden. The deception that I allowed to thrive deep within was the notion that because of my erratic Christian life, God just tolerated me. My perfectionist tendencies had raised the bar to such an impossible level I could not please myself, much less God. Something was needed to confront my heartfelt conviction that in God's eyes I was a huge disappointment. However, I was led to read a book that caused a major shift in the way I saw myself in God's eyes.

When I read Henri Nouwen's *Life of the Beloved*, I readily identified with his vivid depictions of the lies and deceptions that we allow to thrive in our innermost thoughts. Nouwen speaks to the difficulty we have in hearing anything positive about ourselves: "It certainly is not easy to hear that voice [of God] in a world filled with voices that shout: 'You are no good, you are ugly; you are worthless; you are despicable, you are nobody – unless you can demonstrate the opposite.' These voices are so loud and so persistent that it is easy to believe them. That's the trap." I knew I was in that trap and needed a way out.

The way out was provided by an unbelievable statement of affirmation. Nouwen makes a startling claim concerning the words spoken to Jesus at His baptism. As Jesus was coming up out of the water, the heavens were ripped apart and God spoke, "This is my son, the Beloved; my favor rests on him" (Matthew 3:17 NJB). Nouwen argues that these words of God are for *all* humankind, not just for Jesus. This was news to me.

For months I argued with Nouwen. I protested, "Those words were for Jesus, *exclusively!*" But I continued to wrestle with the issue. Then I remembered the most familiar verse in scripture. "For God so loved the *world...*(John 3:16). I could certainly include myself in that group. Then, as I was reading the Gospel of John, I was startled by something in Jesus' high priestly prayer. He prays to His Father that we would know that God loves us (as believers) in the same way that God loved Him (John 17:23). God loves us *the same way* God loved Jesus! My resistance was beginning to wane.

Still, for many months I was not convinced. Oh, I could believe that I was accepted and saved – but not *beloved*. That was going *too far*. I could believe with ease that I was tolerated by God, but certainly not beloved and favored. Some truths are just too large and too wonderful. The great truths are the most difficult to believe.

Slowly, I began to warm up to the possibility that I *was* God's beloved and that God's favor rested upon me. At first this new way of thinking felt uncomfortable, like wearing a large coat that didn't fit. The arms were too long and it seemed to drag the floor. But over time I began to grow into this new way of seeing myself from God's point of view. What really made the difference was the day I began to live "as if" I were God's beloved, "as if" God's favor rested upon me. My focus shifted from my need to *please* God to my need to *trust* God. When I caught myself drifting back to my old ways of thinking, I would gently brush those thoughts aside and quote Matthew's words, "This is my son, the Beloved; my favor rests on him" (3:17 NJB).

And that has made all the difference. Living as God's beloved also changed the way I relate to others. I treat them as if *they* were God's beloved. Seeing them in this new way, I become more caring, accepting and forgiving.

Since I've taken to heart what God says about me, I can affirm that I'm more at peace with myself than I've ever been. There is no compelling need to be busy incessantly. It's okay just to be. I no longer feel like an orphan who is tolerated. Now I'm at home with myself and the caring world around me. I still need to tap down the noisy voices that tell me I'm worthless, that I need to work harder. In those times I find a quiet place where I can hear that other voice that tells me I'm beloved.

When you think of yourself as God's beloved, it can sometimes open a door to an entirely new way of seeing yourself from God's perspective. After all, what is most true about you is what *God says* about you, not what you say about yourself or what others say about you. Therefore, I invite you to consider from scripture—what God says about *you:*

"I have called you by name from the very beginning [a]. You are mine and I am yours [b]. You are my Beloved, on you my favor rests [c]. I have molded you in the depths of the earth and knitted you together in your mother's womb [d]. I have carved you in the palms of my hands and hidden you in the shadow of my embrace [e]. I look at you with infinite tenderness and care for you with a care more intimate than that of a mother for her child [f]." I delight in you and rejoice over you with singing [g]. I will never leave you and nothing will separate us [h]. Even when you are faithless, I am faithful [i]. Because of my infinite love and kindness toward you, what is prepared for you is beyond your most extravagant thought [j].

[a] Revelation 2:17; [b] Jeremiah 31:33; [c] Matthew 3:17; 12:18; [d] Psalms 139:13; [e] Isaiah 49:16; Psalms 36:7; [f] Isaiah 66:13; [g] Zephaniah 3:17; [h] Hebrews 13:5; Romans 8:38-39; [i] Luke 9:41; 1 Corinthians 10:13; [j] 1 Corinthians 2:9.

The Flow of Grace

In the middle of the Twentieth Century ministers and missionaries were burning out in droves. The brightest and best were returning home exhausted mentally and physically. There was sadness in their voices as they told of difficulties encountered and sacrifices made. But worst of all they were depressed and spiritually defeated. The fervor of their conviction was gone, sapping their spirits, chipping away at their hope, making their verdant faith a wasteland.

Dr. Frank Lake, a Christian psychiatrist and a pioneer pastoral counselor, discovered that this highly motivated group was focused on their own merited relationship with God and on *results*. Dr. Lake viewed their zealous efforts "to win approval from God as less a virtue than a neurotic symptom."

Results were important to the Christian workers because whenever there were positive responses to their labors, it gave them a sense of status. And if this sense of status could be sustained over time, they felt that their work was acceptable; and hence, *they* were acceptable. Dr. Lake's diagnosis was that the missionaries were caught in a Cycle of Law. Whenever they were successful, it gave them a sense of status. And if this sense of status could be sustained, they hoped it would lead to acceptance by God. But they could never be good enough or do enough to meet their moralistic expectations. Hence, their goodness and their accomplishments were never enough.

The only cure for this malady was the Cycle of Grace that was based on a model Dr. Frank Lake called the "Dynamic Cycle of Being and Well-being;" it was simply the Cycle of Law in reverse. Instead of beginning with achievement or works and ending with acceptance, Dr. Lake *started* with acceptance. This spiritual progression was later known as:

The Cycle of Grace

Acceptance > Sustenance > Significance > Achievement

Acceptance

This spiritual progression is based on the life of Christ, who from the beginning had a profound sense of God's acceptance. At His baptism as Jesus was coming out of the water, the heavens were ripped apart and Jesus heard the voice of His Father: "This is my beloved Son with whom I am well pleased" (Matthew 3:17). Jesus knew that He was "beloved" by His Father at the outset, and this affirmation shaped the course of His ministry.

Like Christ, your spiritual journey *begins* with a deep sense that you are accepted and beloved because of *who you are* in God's eyes, not the result of anything you've done. Avoiding the trap the missionaries and so many others have fallen into, the main work of your spiritual life is to nurture your identity as God's beloved. It is your true identity. Your motivation and energy to engage in ministry flows from your identity as God's beloved.

Sustenance

In the same way that Jesus drew His strength from God, the Father, so do we. One way to do this is to *sustain* our identity as God's beloved. This is vital because our friends, enemies, colleagues and even family members will try to define our identity for us. In our devotional life we need to soak in our primary identity that we are God's beloved – even in our most difficult days. When Jesus was driven by the Spirit into the wilderness where He was tempted, it was Jesus' identity that was attacked: "If you are the Son of God, convince this stone to become bread" (Luke 4:3).   In subtle and blatant ways our identity as God's beloved will be challenged repeatedly.   Therefore, we need to nurture our relationship with God through the Spirit and the word.

Our identity as God's beloved needs to be the focus of our time alone with God because the knowledge that we are God's beloved needs to travel the long journey from our head to our heart. The challenge is to claim who we really are in Christ and live into that truth. As we cultivate the sense that we are God's beloved, we are better able to brush aside other voices that can lead us away from God's best intention for us.

Again, Jesus is our example. After healing Peter's mother-in-law and later healing many people in the city of Capernaum, Jesus went out early in the morning to a lonely place to pray. When they found Him, they told Jesus, "Everyone is searching for you" (Mark 1:37). Without a moment's hesitation, Jesus said, "Let us go on to the next towns that I may preach there also; for that is why I came out" (Mark 1:38).

As a minister, I have marveled at this story. Like a magnet, I have always been drawn to the needs of people. Unlike Jesus, it would have taken an enormous force of will for me to go to the next town where people did not know me. Legions of pastors are co-dependent and find themselves hopelessly addicted to the approval of others. But Jesus was guided by His identity as God's beloved and found His significance *there*. This gave Jesus the freedom to pursue His destiny even if it meant not meeting the needs of all who sought Him.

A careful reading of the New Testament will reveal a rhythm of withdrawal where Jesus found time alone with His Father. Withdrawal was an integral part of Jesus' life. It was there—apart from the clamor for His healing touch, at a distance from the hurts and pains of others—that He rested in the love, delight and will of His Father. As God's beloved Son, Jesus was drawn, not to the demands of the crowd, but to His Father's will. In that solitary place Jesus found His significance.

As we employ the disciplines of our faith—such as prayer, the study of scripture, worship and the sacraments – they should confirm our identity as God's beloved. Jesus was well versed in scripture and participated in the festivals and Sabbath worship that was His custom. Similarly, we need to avail ourselves of the spiritual resources that are our custom, to the end that we become like "a tree planted by streams of water that brings forth its fruit in its season" (Psalms 1:3). In a disciplined way we need to send our spiritual roots deep into the streams of living water.

Significance

We all have a need to feel that we are important, that we matter, and that we make a difference. The need for significance is so great that it shapes most of the decisions we make. Money, power and prestige, all apparent expressions of significance, are aggressively pursued in our society. So much so that people will lie, steal and even kill for the feeling that they are important, that they are somebody. The ever-present temptation to feel significant, sometimes at a cost to ourselves or to others, nips at our heels all the days of our lives.

The way we pursue significance determines the direction of our lives. As Christians, when we claim our adoption into the family of God, our significance is not found in *what we do* but in *who we are* as God's beloved. As the Spirit bears witness with our spirit that we are children of God, the sense of our kinship with God tempers our need to *strive* for significance. And our identity in Christ shapes the way we find significance. When we settle into the assurance that we are God's beloved, our identity as God's beloved *becomes* the source of our significance. So, we don't need to meet everyone's need or work endlessly for the praises of others. Our significance is found elsewhere – when we see ourselves as the Father sees us.

Achievement

There is an undeniable expectation that the followers of Christ are to bear fruit. John writes in his Gospel, "By this is my Father glorified that you bear much fruit, and so prove to be my disciples" (John 15:8). But, as we have seen, bearing fruit from a misguided motivation can lead to burnout. So, we do good works, *not* to earn God's approval; we do good works because we already have God's favor as His beloved son or daughter. Therefore, we labor in God's vineyard from a sense of gratitude. There is nothing to prove. We are not called to work *for God* but to allow God to work *through us.*

The way God works though us is intensely personal. God calls each of us to do that which is uniquely ours to do. And our greatest satisfaction in life comes from finding and doing God's will. Frederick Buechner affirms that God calls us to work in that place where our gladness and the world's needs meet. The flow of grace is like a lazy river. You can't push it. Each of us has a song to sing in life, something that God desires to accomplish through us. And as we delight ourselves in the Lord, He gives us the desires of our hearts. But we must be patient. When we give ourselves the freedom just to go with the flow of grace, we have to trust that God is at work in our lives, even in the most ordinary of days.

Chapter Seven

GOD'S TRUE NATURE REVEALED

"As I page through those ancient stories [in scripture] from the sunken ease of my living room chair, it is not hard for me to hear in them the echo of God's voice. But can I hear Him now, speaking not to Moses or to David but to me?

Should we even expect him to speak in the everyday moments of our lives? Or should we be content with echoes, however eloquent, from the past?

If God does still speak, perhaps some of those words are for us."

—Ken Gire

God Revealed to Us

As you read the Gospels, you can't miss the unmistakable aroma and sounds of a banquet: a lamb roasting, bread baking, wine being poured, oil on the food, laughter and storytelling amid a feast lovingly prepared. But in the New Testament a banquet is more than a celebration; it is often a metaphor for God's presence with God's people. An invitation to a banquet is an invitation to a relationship with God. The feasting, the joy, the conversation, the intimacy of a meal shared is a picture of what it's like to experience God.

But how *do* we experience God? According to Albert Schweitzer, we experience God in much the same way that the followers of Jesus experienced Him as they walked with Him in Nazareth and the surrounding countryside. They, of course, were able to see Him in person. But after His death, we would expect that all they had were their memories of Him. However, this is not the case. Beyond memory, they experienced the Living Lord in a multitude of ways. And Schweitzer maintains that our Lord comes to us *the same way* He came to His contemporaries:

> He comes to us as One unknown,
> without a name,
> as of old by the lakeside
> he came to those people who knew him not.
> He speaks to us.
> He speaks the same word: 'Follow thou me!'
> and sets us to the tasks which he has to fulfill for our time.
> He commands.
> And those who obey him,
> whether they be wise or simple,
> he will reveal himself
> in the toils, the conflicts, the sufferings which they will pass
> through in his fellowship.
> And,
> as an ineffable mystery,
> they shall learn in their own experience Who he is.

For Schweitzer, as we obey our Lord's call and follow, He reveals His nature to us in our "own experience" amid our turmoil, ambiguities, triumphs and disappointments. But to perceive the hand of God in our lives and see God's relentless love reflected there is not easily discerned, nor is it easily described. It is a mystery difficult to explain. And only as we reflect upon our experience is God revealed to us.

Our Lord's desire is to reveal His nature to us. Jesus said, "...[H]e who loves me will be loved by my Father, and I will love him and *manifest* myself to him" (John 14:21) [Italics added]. We come to know the Lord as we experience Him at work in our lives. As we love and obey Him, He *reveals* some aspect of His nature to us. And sometimes I've been surprised by what's been revealed.

As God Guides, God Reveals

In the Book of Psalms, God's ever-present guiding hand is eloquently portrayed: "If I take the wings of the morning and dwell in the uttermost parts of the sea, even there thy hand shall lead me" (Psalms 139:9-10). From beginning to end, scripture depicts God as one who actively guides people with compassion and love. "I led them with cords of compassion, with bands of love..." (Hosea 11:4). The following individuals or groups were guided by God to accomplish a specific task.

It was God who led Abraham out of the land of Ur to settle in Canaan. God led Moses to confront the Pharaoh to release the Israelites from bondage in Egypt. God led the Israelites in the wilderness with a cloud by day and a pillar of fire by night and the shepherds to Bethlehem. God led Joseph to take his family and flee to Egypt. God led Ruth to glean in the fields of Boaz, and led Esther to risk her life for the lives of her people. God led Peter to take the Gospel to the Gentiles. God led Ananias to meet and anoint Saul of Tarsus who later became Paul the Apostle. All these individuals were led by God to move in a direction that fulfilled God's purpose for that particular time and place. And the manner in which God led individuals or groups revealed God's nature.

Because God is the same yesterday, today and tomorrow, the reality that God actively leads people *today* should not be surprising. Yet, in a way, whenever God's guiding hand is revealed in a person's life, it is not only surprising; it is amazing. As I reflect on two major turning points early in my career, I am humbled because God's guiding hand was evident in both. However, the first instance of God's leading was such an emotionally wrenching experience I did not see the hand of God.

To become a pastoral counselor, six months of clinical experience is required. In order to fulfill this expectation, I served as a chaplain intern at the Georgia Regional Hospital at Atlanta where I worked under the watchful eyes of two clinical supervisors. Toward the end of this experience, Bill Phillips, one of the supervisors, asked me what I was going to do when I completed my time with them. I told him I planned to enter a doctoral program at Emory University in the area of pastoral counseling.

Bill was shocked to hear this. He growled, "You mean to tell me you're going back to school *again?* Edwin, for the last eleven years you've lived in a late adolescent world on a university campus. You don't know *anything* about older people or children.

You don't know *anything* about marriage or death. As matter of fact, you don't know *anything about anything!"*

"That may be true, but I'm still going to Emory," I replied defiantly.

"No you're not."

"You can't stop me!" I shouted.

"Oh yes I can. I'm adjunct faculty at the Candler School of Theology. I'll write the Dean of the Graduate School and tell him your application is self-destructive."

I sat in stunned silence. I knew he would do it. I'd been blocked from pursuing my dream. I seethed with anger. "Who do you think you are!?!" I blurted.

Bill ignored my ranting and in a calm, deliberate voice, said, "I'll tell you what you need to do. You need to go back to South Georgia where your roots are and serve as a pastor in a church. There you will learn about the real world of people – young and old, black and white, saints and sinners. And after a good dose of that, *then* go back to school and become a pastoral counselor."

Our conversation was over.

When I returned home and recounted to my wife my conversation with Bill, the anger and sadness poured out in a torrent of tears. We loved Atlanta. Our idyllic plans and dreams were suddenly inaccessible. All because of one bull-headed, arrogant supervisor! While our emotions were still running high, David, our five-month-old son began to cry in another room. When Carole brought him to us, his behavior caught us off guard. He was joyous. He began to laugh, smile and almost dance. Carole and I were two of the saddest people on the face of the earth and he was the happiest. It was so incongruous. It was as if he were trying to cheer us up, and his laughter was contagious.

Before we knew it, with tears of frustration still in our eyes, we all began to laugh. When he saw us laughing, he laughed all the more and so did we. The scene was comical. After a moment when we could catch our breath, we all held each other in a tight hug. The little person in our midst was reminding us of something important: we were a family. And together we would face our uncertain future.

As much as I hate to admit it, Bill Phillips was right. His advice to return to South Georgia and minister in a local church was exactly where I needed to be. After a while, it was where I *wanted* to be. I served two churches for a total of fourteen years, and during that time earned a doctorate and finished my supervision to become a certified pastoral counselor. This led to a position at the Pastoral Institute in Columbus, Georgia, where a year later, Bill Phillips, my friend and colleague, was invited to speak.

When it was determined that a resource center for clergy was needed at the Pastoral Institute, they tapped me to be the founding director, largely because of my years in parish ministry. Later when the South Georgia Conference of the United Methodist Church was searching for a conference pastoral counselor, I was their choice, again because of my many years in the local church. My parish experience opened *both* doors. However, initially I did not see God at work. Only a closed door. It was later that I recognized the Lord's guiding hand and His kindness in the manner in which I was led.

A Meeting on Holy Ground

Henry Blackaby in *Experiencing God* has a delightful way of describing God's sovereignty over history. He simply says that God is always up to something. Thirty years ago God apparently was up to something at Wesley Monumental United Methodist Church in Savannah. Through an extraordinary chain of events God seemingly plucked me from one church and planted me in another. The extraordinary manner in which this story unfolds says something of the mystery and wonder of God's ways.

My surprise move to Savannah was set in motion by chance meetings with two men in two unlikely places. In 1976 while volunteering at the Jimmy Carter Campaign Headquarters in Plains, Georgia, I ran into Ron Hudspeth, the conference pastoral counselor, who happened to be visiting Plains. Although I was surprised to see him, with some uncertainty I took the opportunity to mention my interest in starting my training as a pastoral counselor. Without a moment's hesitation he said, "Listen, Jason Shirah is at Wesley Monumental Church in Savannah. He's over

there slugging it out all by himself in that huge church. You ought
to go and help him. The two of you would make a great team.
And you can get your training there."

Later that evening I told my wife of my chance meeting
with Ron Hudspeth. We discussed the implications of a move to
Savannah and began to pray about this possibility. A week later on
a sultry Saturday morning in late July, we took our two boys to
Dooly, an old Methodist campground where camp meetings were
held every summer. What actually drew us to that place was the
pool. We wanted our boys to enjoy the water while Carole and I
talked about our future. After a forty-minute drive, we were all in
the pool. We had the place to ourselves. We discussed the
possibility of taking a trip to Savannah to look the place over.

Our boys had splashed in the pool for about an hour when I
noticed a blue Buick drive onto the grounds. From a distance the
figure that emerged from the car looked like Jason Shirah, the
pastor of Wesley Monumental Church in Savannah. But I wasn't
sure. When he arrived at the pool, he extended his hand and

warmly greeted us, "Jason Shirah. It's good to see you, Edwin, and this must be Carole."

After introducing our visitor to our two boys, looking directly at Jason, I asked Carole, "Guess we should tell him that we've been talking about him all morning?"

When I told Jason of my interest in joining him in ministry at Wesley Monumental, he was astounded. With a dazed look he hung on every word. When I finished, he turned the tables on me, "Let me tell you *the rest of the story,*" he said. "I tried to have you appointed to Wesley in June but was blocked by your District Superintendent who insisted you were needed where you were. So I had to drop the matter."

At this point we realized that our unplanned rendezvous that morning at Dooly Campground was much more than a coincidence. Jason paused, looked toward the open air tabernacle and said, "You know, I grew up in Byromville, not far from this campground and drove by here this morning to pray."

For a moment we sat in silence trying to comprehend all that had been said and the unlikely chance of our meeting that morning at Dooly. We were experiencing what Jason later described as the strongest example of God's providence he had ever experienced. And Carole and I could say the same. Jason had traveled almost 200 miles from the east and we had driven thirty miles from the west and met each other at a remote campground in southwest Georgia. The statistical likelihood of our meeting that morning in that place would have been minuscule!

When Jason told the bishop of our "chance meeting" at Dooly Campground, the bishop responded, "You got him!" In those three words the bishop was saying: "This is the hand of God. I'm not standing in the way." We moved to Savannah two months later.

When I recall these events I can only shake my head and wonder: what kind of God is this who orchestrates such a dramatic coincidence? Frederick Buechner has suggested that God uses such coincidences to get our attention. These days whenever I encounter a coincidence draped in a mystic weave I look for the hand of God and lift a prayer of thanksgiving.

A Delightful Side of God

A unique characteristic of the Judeo-Christian faith is that God actually *speaks* to people. The first sentence in the Book of Hebrews states that God spoke in the past through prophets "but in these last days" God spoke through His Son (Hebrews 1:1). God speaks and interacts, not only with prophets, but with ordinary people.

Something happened at the University of Connecticut in the spring of 1971 that gives undeniable evidence that God speaks today with clarity and authority. But on this occasion what was revealed was an unexpected and delightful side of God. In an amazing demonstration of God's power and savvy, the events of that extraordinary evening unfolded like something straight from the Book of Acts.

At the beginning of spring quarter, a man in his thirties with a full beard and dressed in a flowing white robe appeared on campus claiming to be the return of Christ. His name was Jesus

Julius. He was always accompanied by a group of loyal followers, some of whom had mortgaged their homes to support him financially. Jesus Julius was tall, handsome and articulate.

As I was walking across campus on a beautiful spring morning, I was met by a group of students involved in our Campus Crusade ministry. They informed me that I was scheduled to debate Jesus Julius in the student center that evening at eight o'clock. That was the first I had heard of this. Although I was seminary trained, I was no candidate for the debate team. Debating from scripture was hardly my forte. I prepared as best I could, reviewing selected scriptures on the return of Christ.

That evening about 150 students gathered in the student center. On the stage was a table, several chairs and two microphones. The largest student meeting on that campus the previous year was a presentation on witchcraft. The University of Connecticut in those years had become a battleground for the minds and hearts of students.

Twenty minutes into the debate my worst fears were realized. When I challenged Julius with a scripture that I was certain would discredit him, he just smiled as if he'd anticipated the question; then he gave an eloquent defense that threw me off balance. I would respond by saying something like "Really?" or "That's interesting." Needless to say, Jesus Julius took charge of the debate early and was by far the dominant voice. To be honest, he was mopping the floor with me.

In frustration I handed the microphone to a colleague and told him to take over. I made my way out a side door to the parking lot to pray. If this debate did not turn around soon, many students were going to be confused or, worse, misled into following an impostor. Leaning against the side of a car, I earnestly poured out my heart to God: "Lord, help me. You know he's a fraud; I know he's a fraud, but these students don't know. Lord, the Baal worshipers were frauds and you exposed them. Do it again. Show me the way."

Not knowing what to expect, I waited in silence. And in a way I cannot explain, I was given the words, "Look at him closely." And standing in the parking lot, I looked to heaven as if to say, "And...?" But there was only silence. "Look at him closely" was the unmistakable answer to my prayer. The challenge was to trust what I'd been given.

I returned to the student center and waited in the wings just long enough to discern that Jesus Julius was still firmly in control of the debate. I returned to the stage and moved my chair closer to get a better look at this Jesus figure. As my colleague bantered back and forth with him, I was praying silently, "Lord, I'm looking at his face. I'm looking at his beard and neck. I'm looking at his arms, his hands." Then something caught my attention. And I began to reflect on what I saw.

When there was a lull in the dialogue, I pulled the microphone close to me and speaking as clearly as possible, I asked, "Jesus, when you walked the earth the first time, did you have the peace of God that passes all understanding? Did you ever worry? Were you ever anxious?"

"No, I am always at peace."

"And as you walk the earth today, do you have the peace of God? Do you ever worry?"

"As I said, I'm *always* at peace."

"Well, I notice that you bite your fingernails."

When I said this, he was taken aback. He held up both hands chest high and looked down at his nails as if to see them for the first time. And, in doing so, he displayed to the students on the front row his hideous looking red and swollen fingertips. Just then a booming voice from the back of the auditorium demanded, *"Does* he bite his nails?"

And someone on the front row turned and shouted back, "Down to the nubs!"

This brought a roar of laughter. Then like a wave, a murmur moved through the audience. Slowly, students began to stand and some shaking their heads began walking toward the doors in the back of the room. We watched in awe as the students gradually vacated the building. After a few moments the only people remaining in the auditorium were some friends of mine, a man in a robe and a group of his followers.

The debate was over. The next day Jesus Julius left town.

That fateful evening the Lord revealed His power, but also something else – His mirth. There was something comical about what had happened. Jesus Julius was exposed, not for lack of biblical knowledge or his skill as a debater, but because the audience soundly rejected a Jesus who bites his fingernails!

When the dust settled, there was no doubt that the spirit of God had been at work in our midst in a powerful way. Into the night the students and I talked and reflected on what had taken place. We laughed, told the story over and over and gave God the glory. We experienced a God who laughs and at times causes us mortals to laugh (Psalms 2:4; Genesis 17:17). We were struck with the awesome power of God who in an instant can turn an embarrassing defeat into an unexpected victory.

Schweitzer promised that in our trials, our Lord would reveal *who He is* in our own experience. This is precisely what had taken place. That evening the Lord revealed to a small group of believers His power and the wonder of His ways. And sometimes God's ways are so outlandish they cause us to laugh. With an economy of words, the Living Lord revealed to us Jesus Julius' place of vulnerability, and like a surprise move in a chess game, used it to checkmate an imposter.

Since that time, whenever I sing Martin Luther's great hymn, "A Mighty Fortress Is Our God," I always recall the debate. In one couplet Luther captures that evening:

> And though this world, with devils filled,
> should threaten to undo us....
> The Prince of Darkness grim, we tremble not for him...
> one little word shall fell him.

A Likable God

When Philip Yancey asked himself what he thought he would have noticed about Jesus had Yancey lived in the First Century, he said he would have noticed that Jesus was *likable*. For Yancey, the Gospels present Jesus as "a man who has such charisma that people will sit three days straight without food, just to hear his riveting words." Unlike other religious leaders, Jesus taught with disarming authority. His everyday, tersely-told stories were unforgettable. A servant who was supposed to invest his master's money buries it instead. A selfish judge fearing a black eye from a pestering widow gives her justice. People not only loved these stories, they were drawn to the storyteller, so much so that sinners heard Him gladly. Jesus, the winsome and down to earth teacher,

drew crowds so large that His enemies said of Him, "...[T]he
world has gone after him" (John 12:19).

More than anyone, I believe Philip Yancey has identified
what made Jesus so likable. In addition to being in touch with a
broad range of feelings, Jesus could reach out and affirm others.
He was personable; He could quickly establish intimacy with a
stranger. We see this in His encounters with a Samaritan woman, a
tax-collector named Zaccheus, and a woman caught in adultery.
Centuries ahead of His time, Jesus was sensitive to the needs of
women and children. Yancey sums up what he would have noticed
about Jesus this way:

> Jesus was "the man for others," in Bonhoeffer's fine
> phrase. He kept himself free– free for the other person.
> He would accept almost anybody's invitation for
> dinner, and as a result no public figure had a more
> diverse list of friends, ranging from rich people, Roman
> centurions and Pharisees to tax collectors, prostitutes,
> and leprosy victims. People *liked* being with Jesus;
> where he was, joy was.

If God is the same yesterday, today and tomorrow, it stands
to reason that this likable side of God would shine through even
today. Our Lord's likableness may already be present in our

dealings with Him, but our earth-bound expectations may limit our ability to perceive it. Just as I was directed to look for God's love and kindness in everyday events, the challenge may be to look for God's likableness in the same place.

If we looked for it, we just might see something likable about a God who cradles children in His arms and blesses them, takes up for children and can see the world through the eyes of children. There is something noble about a Savior who, to the dismay of fellow Jews, always delights in a demonstration of great faith, even if that person is a Roman Centurion, a Samaritan or some other foreigner. There is something likable about a Savior who in the midst of a storm falls asleep in the back of a small boat, and when awakened calms the waves then uses the whole scenario as a teaching moment for His disciples. There is something endearing about a God who takes great pleasure in a recitation of outlandish excuses and recognizes something marvelous in a poor widow's gift.

And in my experience, there is something likable about a Lord who employs extraordinary means to demonstrate His love and kindness. There is something delightful about a God who exposes a Jesus impersonator because the impostor bites his fingernails! There is something wonderful about a God who orchestrates a pastoral move by bringing two ministers together in a place so remote that there could be a sign posted that reads, "This ain't the end of the world, but you can see it from here." Who wouldn't like a God such as this?

A God Who Likes You

While reading the works of the desert monks, Roberta Bondi was surprised to discover that "God actually liked us." When Sally Field received her Emmy Award in 2007, she held it up and proclaimed, "You like me. You really like me!" The sound of surprise in her voice was palpable. I think we are often surprised when we are told that someone likes us. If this is true on a human level, no wonder we have difficulty believing it when we hear that God likes us – that God really likes us!

Should we be surprised that God likes us? Consider the biblical record. Sinners rallied to Jesus for two reasons: They liked Him and *He liked them*. There is little doubt that Jesus liked

what He saw in the life and character of the rich young ruler. And,

according to the Gospel writers, Jesus was very fond of Peter,

James and John, who were part of His inner circle. These three

disciples accompanied Him to the Mount of Transfiguration and

remained by His side during Jesus' agonizing hours in the Garden

of Gethsemane.

Another group of close friends resided in Capernaum.

Jesus was a frequent visitor in the home of Lazarus and his two

sisters; and the tone of their conversations indicated that of a close

friendship. Jesus liked them and they liked Him. When Jesus

heard of the death of His friend Lazarus, Jesus wept. When the

question was asked as to why Jesus wept, Frederick Buechner

explained it this way:

> Why does he weep? The narrative tells us that the
> people standing around him said that it was because he
> loved Lazarus, and it is not hard to believe that that
> was part of it. Lazarus is the only friend the Gospels
> name who does not seem to have been a disciple
> especially but just a friend, somebody he didn't have to
> be the messiah with maybe but could just be himself
> with, somebody to have a drink with once in a while, to
> tell what it was like to be himself. Lazarus was his

friend, and he loved him, so now that he was dead, Jesus wept - for his friend and wept for himself who would have to face the music from now on without his friend.

It is expected that God would love us because God is love. But for God to *like* us, to be drawn to us as Webster's Dictionary says by "varying degrees of attraction" is *not* expected. Some would argue that for God to like us is more powerful than for God to love us. This is because "love" has been so trivialized in our culture the word no longer evokes strong feelings. A friend of mine recently told me, "I love Diet Coke." Now he doesn't really *love* the diet beverage, he just *prefers* it. When a teenager was looking for just the right Valentine card, the clerk suggested a card that said, "To the *only* girl I've ever loved." The teenager said, "That's perfect! I'll take *four*."

Because the word "love" has been so diminished; the word "like" carries a freshness that touches us at a different place. In families, we are obliged to love each other; but not to like each other. When we hear that God likes us, we respond because beyond God's love for us, it is God's good pleasure to like us. And a God who likes us is naturally likable.

Once you've experienced the love of a likable God, there is a tendency to want to share this love. One of the hallmarks of God's love is the desire to love others: "We love, because he first loved us" (1 John 4:19). Love is never to be hoarded, but is to be released into the world where it can transform people like Saul – a persecutor of Christians – into Paul the Apostle, who loved deeply and in his letter to the Corinthians taught others to do the same. God is the motivation to love others *and* is the source of that love. But the connection between our love for one another and God's love for us is hidden. In the next chapter we will explore the hidden source of love's power.

Chapter Eight

LOVE'S HIDDEN POWER

"We want only to show you something we have seen and to tell you something we have heard...that here and there in the world and now and then in ourselves is a new creation."

—Paul Tillich

Love's Hidden Power

Søren Kierkegaard, always fascinated by the way God's love empowers how we love one another, illustrates this with a pastoral metaphor: "As the quiet lake is fed deep down by the flow of hidden springs, which no eye sees, so a human being's love is grounded, still more deeply in God's love." Love possesses a hidden restorative power that cannot be seen on the surface.

When we look beneath the surface of our relationships with one another, we may ask: How is our love grounded in God's love? More specifically, how does God's relentless love touch the

way we believe, hope and endure? To explore this, I suggest we
return to Paul's statement in First Corinthians 13:7.

> "Love believes all things,
>   Hopes all things,
>   Endures all things."

As we have seen, love does not exist exclusively on a
human level. It is always preceded by God's love. It is shaped by
God's work in the world, a work proclaimed in three succinct
statements found in the communion ritual of the Roman Catholic
Church and in that of several Protestant denominations: the United
Methodist Church, the Episcopal Church and the Presbyterian
Church, U.S.A. Toward the end of the liturgy there is a response
the worshipers either sing or recite:

> "Christ has died.
>   Christ is risen.
>   Christ will come again."

When we place these affirmations alongside Paul's words
in First Corinthians, something unexpected emerges:

Because Christ has died, we can *believe* all things.

Because Christ is risen, we can *hope* all things.

Because Christ will come again, we can *endure* all things.

These three statements reveal the source of love's hidden power. Reflecting on them is like looking beneath the surface of Kierkegaard's lake and seeing for the first time the countless springs that feed it. In essence, the source of love's power is grounded in Christ's death, resurrection and promised return.

Because Christ Has Died, We Can Believe All Things

"Christ has died," stated in the *past tense*, anchors the life of Christ in history. This is important because our faith is grounded in historical fact, not fantasy or myth.

At the outset, let me say that the connection between Christ's death and how that helps us believe all things was not obvious at first. However, further reflection brought to light several connections that are theologically viable. Like the springs of Kierkegaard's lake, the spiritual source of our believing was hidden.

First, Jesus lived out what has become the linchpin of all theological discourse: the cross. Our Lord's death on the cross is the central moment in which we see the love of God that believes the best in us, displayed against the hatred of the world that believes the worst.

The death of Christ reveals God's love for us. Paul states in Romans that "while we were still sinners, Christ died for us" (Romans 5:8 NIV). In other words, while we were in rebellion against God, Christ believed in us enough to die for us. And the words that Jesus spoke from the cross give evidence that this is true. When He said, "Father, forgive them for they know not what they do," Jesus graciously gave the benefit of the doubt to those who were crucifying Him and offered them a mediating excuse. We believe the best concerning one another because on the cross Christ believed the best concerning us. As followers of Christ, the challenge is to do the same to those who persecute us.

In *Les Misérables*, Victor Hugo spends fifty pages describing the character of the bishop. This extraordinary person was so convinced of God's love and kindness that he poured out that kindness on the poor and needy. When the thief Jean Valjean showed up at his door, it was second nature for the bishop to surprise this unsavory character with an extravagant gift because on the cross Christ had already surprised the bishop with His gift of love – His life. The bishop believed all things concerning Valjean because the bishop knew that Christ believed all things concerning him.

Secondly, when Christ died on the cross, He identified completely with the worst in us, and we were identified with the best in Him. Paul says it this way: "For our sake He made Him to be sin who knew no sin, so that in Him we might become the righteousness of God" (2 Corinthians 5:21). Martin Luther called this "the great exchange." In this divine exchange Christ takes upon Himself our sin and we are given His righteousness. In this way God makes us righteous.

When we comprehend this gracious truth for ourselves, we are better able to see others as righteous in God's eyes. This paves the way for us, like Victor Hugo's bishop, to believe the best concerning the thieves and scoundrels who cross *our* path. But notice that this new way of seeing people has its origin in the cross. Therefore, we can say with certainty that Christ's death empowers us to believe all things.

Because Christ Is Risen, We Can Hope All Things

"Christ is risen," stated in the *present tense*, describes a Living Lord who gives us a living hope. Although it looks like we live in a Good Friday world where pain and death have the last word, hope is present in every moment. But it is hidden, for hope is the expectation of things not seen.

Whenever we speak of our hope in Christ, our hope must have a solid foundation lest it be dismissed as mere wishful thinking. For the writer of Luke-Acts, hope derives its power from the victory over death made possible through the resurrection. That is why Paul, when making his defense before King Agrippa, states that his hope stands or falls on the resurrection of Christ (Acts 26:8).

Because of the resurrection, our hope is unshakable and entitles us to a boldness and a freedom that stand up to disappointments, trials, and sufferings. Vaclav Havel, President of the Czech Republic, describes hope as a radical way of believing. For him, hope is not believing that we can change something; it's believing that our efforts matter. In our struggles against injustice, oppression and prejudice, Havel is saying that what we do in the name of Christ is never wasted because ultimately death will be swallowed up in life.

Our hope in Christ is a call to courageous action. There is no excuse for sitting on the sidelines. The challenge is to be "the resurrection" to a hurting world. Christ calls us to bring resurrection-hope to a despairing world. Christ's resurrected life is in us waiting to be unleashed. Far from wishful thinking, this living hope is grounded in a truth we proclaim in worship: "Christ is risen."

Because Christ Will Come Again, We Can Endure All Things

"Christ will come again," stated in the *future tense*, points to a future event that already impacts the present moment.

Across the centuries, when Christians have faced persecution, the belief in Christ's return has brought strength and comfort. "If we endure, we shall also reign with him" (2 Timothy 2:12). The belief that Christ will come again assures us of His love, especially in times of suffering. When we feel beaten down by our circumstances or persecutors, the belief that Christ will come again stirs up our courage, and helps us to endure. God's announcement of Christ's return tells us ahead of time what's coming in order to encourage us in the present.

There is always the risk that our sacrifices and sufferings will be for naught. The awful prospect that evil may ultimately triumph lurks in the shadows and at times bursts forth and all but overwhelms us. At such times only a Messiah can help us endure. When He comes, He will wipe away all tears, He will do away with pain and death. He will dwell with us in a New Jerusalem (Isaiah 25:6). The hope that He who came will come again sustains us and helps us to endure even the darkest of days. But we are helped to endure only if we choose to see a situation from God's perspective, a worldview that includes meaning and purpose.

When I was a sophomore in college, I spent two months in Poland on a student exchange program. I was not prepared for what awaited me there. The group I was with took a half-day train ride to a place that still makes me shudder inside when I think about it forty-seven years later. The place was Auschwitz, the concentration camp I referred to earlier in the text. At every turn there were reminders of unspeakable suffering, misery and death. However, Viktor Frankl, a psychiatrist, not only survived the horrors of Auschwitz, but did so because he refused to abandon all that was good and hopeful while braving the worst conditions conceivable.

Frankl observed that people could endure suffering if there appeared to be some meaning to it, but were overwhelmed by meaningless suffering. He discovered that finding meaning in terrible situations did not make the pain go away; but it made the pain *tolerable*. For Frankl, the meaning of our lives is not invented or created by ourselves. The meaning is already there waiting to be detected. The meaning is there, yet hidden.

The same was true for Joseph, who for years toiled as a slave of the Egyptians, having been sold into slavery by his brothers (Genesis 43-45). For decades this cruel betrayal must have felt like a meaningless act of vengeance. A careful reading of this story reveals that Joseph may have toyed with the idea of taking revenge against his brothers. But Joseph finally discovered that God's purposes were being worked out through those awful years of slavery and imprisonment. He told his brothers later that what they intended for evil, God used for the saving of countless lives (Genesis 45:5-7). This was the meaning of his suffering; but it was hidden for many years. And after the passage of so much time, it is remarkable that Joseph was still open to discern the meaning that was there.

Joseph, like Viktor Frankl, had every reason to indulge himself in bitterness and hatred. However, both men, separated by centuries, chose to see their suffering from God's perspective. When we find ourselves in a situation where we can do nothing, we may choose bitterness or we can live in the hope that someday the meaning of it will be revealed. Frankl places the challenge before us: "When we are no longer able to change a situation – we are challenged to change ourselves."

When James Carroll, a Catholic priest, found himself depressed and despairing in a jail cell back in 1972, he was empowered to transform his perspective by what he heard coming from another cell. He had been arrested for trespassing at the U. S. Capitol as part of an anti-war protest. There were two dozen or so prisoners in separate cells, all of whom had been part of the demonstration against the Viet Nam War. The group, mostly ministers and priests, waited in silence as the hours dragged by in agonizing slow motion.

Father Carroll, depressed and afraid, was thinking about all that had taken place to bring him to this low moment. Then a man in the next cell began to sing. His deep baritone voice filled the emptiness of the night. The man was singing Handel's *Messiah:* "Comfort ye, comfort ye, my people." Father Carroll recognized the voice as that of William Sloan Coffin, the spokesman of the group. Soon others joined in and Carroll followed along as best he could: "The people that walked in darkness have seen a great light." For the priest, the music became a prayer; he could feel his fears subsiding, his resolve returning. He recalls:

> As you listened to Coffin—"And we like sheep, and we like sheep, and we like sheep—have gone astray," you suddenly felt awash in unexpected gratitude, for you

realized that those words expressed your deepest faith, and that sung as they were, these words had an absolute integrity that far transcended your fearful hesitance. You did believe that your Redeemer liveth, and, more than that, you believed that your Redeemer had stood upon the earth with you, bringing you to that most unlikely place. You saw, indeed, that you belonged there, in that cell block, and that you were plenty strong enough for whatever lay ahead.

When the singing subsided, James Carroll's belief in what he was doing was stronger than ever – as was his hope that his time in that jail cell would make a difference in the world. All he did was sing. And the words and the melody, celebrating the coming of the Messiah, created a new reality—one conducive to enduring a miserable night and the long days ahead with an undeniable sense of purpose. Because Christ will come again, we can endure *all* things.

The hope of a coming Messiah not only helps us endure, His coming heralds the great celebration, the Feast of the Lamb, a celebration of the final victory over the forces of evil. The sound of a celebration is one of the hallmarks of God's Kingdom.

Chapter Nine

A JOYOUS CELEBRATION

"Jesus came and wherever he went there was a party....Or there was a party and Jesus was there."

—Karl Olsson

Celebrating the Kingdom

Some celebrations are unforgettable. When Karl Olsson was no more than six years of age, he attended a Christmas party that took place in a room adjacent to his uncle's grocery store. The aroma of cheese and coffee filled the air. The room, lit with candles as there was no electricity, gave a golden glow to the festivities. In the midst of Christmas carols and games too complicated for him, Olsson recalls the bliss of the party.

> I loved the laughing – the red faces, the roars and shrieks. But my most vivid impression was of a young girl – fourteen or fifteen – with hair the color of wheat and a dress of blue velvet. In some game that was passing me by she rescued me. She picked me up and put me in her lap.

I am sure there was something in her act which spoke to my childhood sexuality. It was important to me that she was a girl in blue velvet, blond and tender, but there were other feelings. She made me feel that I belonged to her. Because of her, I felt that I belonged at the party. Something truly beautiful, warm, and human flowered in me. I was happy to be myself, happy to be a boy, and happy to be where I was.

The Bible is filled with stories of parties, lavish festive occasions, where wine flows freely, where guests don special garments and eat delicious, exotic foods. These celebrations point to something beyond: God's Kingdom, the rule of God in the hearts of people. The Kingdom is often portrayed as a party of merriment with music, laughter, dancing and feasting. For that matter, the Bible concludes with an invitation to a party, to the great celebration:

Happy are those who wash their robes clean! They will have the right to the tree of life, and will enter by the gates of the city. 'I, Jesus, have sent my angel to you with this testimony for the churches. I am the root and scion of David, the bright morning star.' 'Come!' say the Spirit and the bride 'Come!' Let each hearer reply. Come! Come forward, you who are thirsty; accept the water of life, a free gift for all who desire it (Rev. 22:14; 16-17, NEB).

With the coming of the Kingdom, scripture paints a picture of an outlandish celebration with the sound of God's trumpets blaring and angels singing. Jesus gives us a glimpse of the celebration in a series of parables spoken to a group of religious leaders.

Three parables in Luke's Gospel picture God pursuing the lost, followed by a huge celebration. The parables were given in response to a complaint muttered by a group of scribes and Pharisees upset that Jesus ate with sinners (Luke 15:2). In response, Jesus tells the parable of the lost sheep, the lost coin, and the lost son. The three parables signify the isolation and separation that accompanies a fractured relationship. These parables give us a picture of God's love that relentlessly searches for us in our pain and grief, and when found, restores us and celebrates over us.

In each parable there are two distinct scenes. The first scene is that of an all-out search and the second is that of an all-out celebration. In the first parable a shepherd has lost a sheep. The picture Jesus paints is that of a shepherd searching all day or longer for that one missing sheep. The second parable is that of a woman who turns her house upside down searching for a lost drachma. In the third, the father of the prodigal son constantly scans the horizon hoping for a glimpse of his lost son. In these three parables God's relentless love is such that God will not rest until the lost is found. The message is clear – what has been lost matters to God.

When the lost has been found, the second scene is that of a party. Henri Nouwen's description of this scene captures the celebratory mood:

> In all three of the parables...God rejoices and invites others to rejoice with him. "Rejoice with me," the shepherd says, "I have found my sheep that was lost." "Rejoice with me," the woman says, "I have found the drachma that was lost." "Rejoice with me," the father says, "this son of mine that was lost is found."
>
> All these are the voices of God. God does not want to keep his joy to himself. He wants everyone to share in it. God's joy is the joy of his angels and his saints; it is the joy of all who belong to the Kingdom.

An inspiring description of God celebrating with His people is given by the prophet Zephaniah. It is a celebration of the coming of God's Kingdom, a time when God reigns in the hearts of all people. "There, in the streets of Jerusalem, are the faithful people of God holding carnival – shouting out their joy to one another, exulting with dance and timbrel and laughter over the fact

that God rules in their lives" (Zephaniah 3:14; Zechariah 9:9;

Isaiah 54:1).

Amid the celebration, the prophet gives a picture of God

rejoicing over His people:

> "He will take great delight in you,
> he will quiet you with his love,
> he will rejoice over you with singing."
> (Zephaniah 3:17 NIV)

According to the prophet, God joins the party, rejoicing and

singing right along with the faithful. God's love is such that God

delights in them and rejoices with them.

But when does all this take place? Most people think of the

Kingdom of God as sometime in the future. For them, the

Kingdom will be revealed at the end of history. This is true, but

there is more to the story. When Jesus taught His disciples to pray

for the Kingdom to come, Jesus was praying for the Kingdom to

come *in its fullness* because the Kingdom was already a present

reality. Jesus also taught that the Kingdom was "at hand;" that it

was within them or in their midst (Luke 17:21).

God reigns in the lives of His people today. And here and there when we stumble upon His presence, power and grace, we celebrate. Some may protest, asking how can we celebrate and invite people to the party at a time when there is so much suffering in the world. The answer lies in the teachings of Jesus, especially His parables.

Almost two-thirds of the parables refer to the Kingdom of God and give us important clues about God's life among us. In the parable of "the hidden treasure" the man sells all he has and buys a field (Matthew 13:44). From this parable we learn that the Kingdom is valuable, and once discovered, must be acquired at some sacrifice. The parable is filled with action words: He *finds*, *sells*, *goes* and *buys*. All this frenetic activity is centered in one thing – God's action and loving presence among us. When we actively love God and neighbor, we "are not far from the kingdom of God" (Mark 12:32-34).

In response to God's love, our love *finds* what God is doing in the world, *buys* into God's redemptive work and *pursues* the lost, the hungry, the outcast. Our response to God's love is not passive. Just the opposite. It actively engages the world at the point of its greatest need and turns the house upside down, searches all night, digs in a field, then calls the neighbors to a party and celebrates like there's no tomorrow.

You see, all this celebrating is *a celebration of love's triumph*. "Love," Paul says, "never fails" (1 Corinthians 13:8). Governments will fail, economies will fail, civilizations will disappear, but God's love will never end. God's love is stronger than death. And that is what the party is all about.

Jesus said, "In this world you will have tribulation."

That's expected.

But then he says, "Be of good cheer, I have overcome the world" (John 16:33).

That's unexpected. And that's the reason we rejoice.

The world began with a magnificent creation and will end with a great celebration. But the reality is that we must live our lives amid all the turmoil and chaos that takes place in these days *between* creation and the coming of the Kingdom. Thankfully, no matter how dark the day, the promise of God's Kingdom still shines within us, around us and before us. All we have to do is trust it.

No matter how confusing our circumstances, the promise of the Kingdom encourages us to live boldly, *trusting* in God's love. In the next chapter we will focus on some practical ways to respond to God's love so that our walk with God in this "in between time" will be authentic, vital and rewarding.

Chapter Ten

A FRESH GLIMPSE OF GOD

"Oh taste and see that the Lord is good!"

—Psalms 34:8

Keeping Your Faith Focused

If your desire is to experience God's love, you have to respond by faith. As God's relentless love keeps coming toward you in countless ways, to say "yes," and *trust* in God's love – is an important act of faith. However, such a step doesn't happen all at once. Your faith journey, more than likely, will have many twists and turns. For most people faith development takes training and practice, like preparing for a long-distance race, which the writer of Hebrews says is run with a disciplined focus:

"...[L]et us run with perseverance the race marked out for us. Let us fix our eyes on Jesus, the author and perfecter of our faith..." (Hebrews 12:1-2 NIV).

Just as a runner concentrates on the finish line, so we look with intensity at Jesus who is the "author" and the "perfecter" of our faith. Jesus is the author of our faith. This means that as we focus our attention on Jesus, He activates or brings our faith alive.

As a senior at Emory University, my faith was enlivened in an unexpected way one evening in a gymnasium. This happened the same year that a professor on the faculty made headlines across the nation by repeating a statement made famous by Friedrick Nietzche that "God is Dead." However, at that same time on Emory's campus a quiet revival was taking place in the hearts of students, replacing their emptiness and cynicism with new life, purpose and joy. I was one of those students.

After saying no four times to a friend, who kept inviting me to various student "gatherings," the fifth time I actually said yes. I consented to attend a weekend retreat. I was curious and intrigued about all that was happening on campus. I went reluctantly to the Campus Crusade Bible study. My attitude was horrible. I figured that the party animals from UGA and the slide-ruler gang from Georgia Tech might be taken in by all this hype about Jesus, but I knew better. I'd taken some religious courses at Emory. I should have checked my pride and arrogance at the door.

The Bible study that evening centered on the man born blind depicted in the ninth chapter of the Gospel of John. With my arms tightly folded across my chest providing a safe barrier between me and the speaker, under my breath, I whispered with cynicism dripping, "Okay, mister, impress me." What I wasn't prepared for was the speaker's gift of humor. With it, he disarmed me. Not fifteen minutes into his talk I was laughing so hard with tears in my eyes, I could barely catch my breath. No longer defiant, I was using my arms to hold me in my chair.

The speaker explained that after Jesus had healed the man's eyes, the Pharisees couldn't understand how an ordinary street preacher could heal a man born blind. The speaker's description of the Pharisees' interrogation of the poor man was nothing short of hilarious. Their arrogance had blinded them to the point of absurdity.

Then something caught my attention. The teacher said that Jesus, when He heard that the Pharisees had thrown the man born blind out of the synagogue, went looking for him. What? The Savior of the world was walking the streets of Jerusalem looking for a lowly blind man He had healed!?! What kind of Savior is this? Suddenly it hit me like a freight train: I saw myself as a Pharisee blinded by *my own* pride. I was a blind man needing the Savior's touch. Just beneath my arrogant bravado was a gnawing emptiness. Maybe this Jesus would come looking for me.

My first prayer was, "Lord, you can find me if you want to." Then I prayed, "Lord, *I want* to be found." Finally, I prayed, "Lord, *I need* to be found." And I was found that night. Without any fanfare, very quietly Christ came into my life. I knew something was different, but I couldn't name it. There was a peace and a joy, and the emptiness was gone as was the arrogance. Gratitude had taken its place. And I can say that over the years God has given me a life more abundant than I could have ever imagined.

That evening Jesus was the author of my faith. At that time my spiritual journey began and over time Christ has become the perfecter of my faith. But my growth in Christ has not taken place in a haphazard manner. The writer of Hebrews is very specific about how this happens. Our faith is developed as we have our eyes firmly fixed on Jesus. In this way Jesus becomes the author *and* perfecter of our faith.

The imperative to keep our eyes fixed on Jesus may sound elementary or so obvious that it does not need mentioning. But there are many distractions. Our fears, our disappointments, our addictions, or our pursuit of wealth can cause our focus to be misplaced. We are also cautioned not to idolize the men and women of faith who have shaped our lives, but to keep our eyes fixed on Jesus. The distractions are so pervasive that the race requires perseverance. The goal is to live our lives fulfilling God's purpose for us. We, as Christians, do this by keeping our eyes intently focused on Jesus. In this way the author of our faith will bring our faith to completion.

Finally, if we are to experience God's love, we need to be open to new perceptions of God. One of the major themes of this book is the way we project onto God old worn-out images and perceptions. And, as they say in politics, "perception is everything." Even if a perception is wrong or faulty, a perception

has the power to pull us toward or push us away from a person or

an idea. The same is true for the way we perceive God. For

Brennan Manning, our perception of God is such an important part

of our spiritual life, he does not mince words:

> Old perceptions of God are difficult to change. They
> have been with us for so long they do not yield easily. If
> we do not allow Jesus to change our perception of God,
> if we continue to cling to our pre-Christian images and
> distorted projections, if we think that Jesus is not easy to
> get along with (is touchy, unapproachable, easily
> annoyed or offended), we reject the gift of his friendship,
> disdain the open airy, spacious atmosphere of his
> Kingdom, and opt for the dark and dreary dungeon of
> distrust.

We must allow fresh new images of God to grow in us like

seeds planted. And the new images must be carefully nourished

and cultivated. When I was learning to see myself as God's

beloved, I wrote the affirmation on a piece of paper and placed it

on my mirror so I would see it first thing every morning. After

many months the old notion that I was merely tolerated by God

faded and was replaced by the refreshing and life-giving thought that I was beloved. After a while it was more than a thought; it had become a heart-felt conviction.

God's love has a way of meeting us where we need it the most. During a time in my life when I was tormented by anxiety and worry, I was led to a passage of scripture where Jesus invites us to deal with our worries and exhaustion by taking on His yoke. As Jesus describes the yoke, He is describing Himself. For me, it was a timely and compelling perception of God:

"Come to me, all who labor and are heavy laden, and I will give you rest. Take my yoke upon you, and learn of me; for I am gentle and lowly in heart, and you will find rest for your souls. For my yoke is easy and my burden is light" (Matthew 11:28-30).

Every Jew listening to this knew that Jesus was referring to the law, that massive body of statutes that faithful Jews were expected to obey. Today it's the pressure to conform, to be respected, to succeed, and the rules are just as elaborate. Because so many people are overwhelmed with anxiety and stress, this scripture gives us a new and refreshing perception of God.

The first image we are offered is that Jesus *cares* that we are weary from the heavy burdens we carry. Jesus invites us to come to Him, to shift our focus and learn of Him. What we learn is that He is gentle and humble of heart for His yoke is easy and His burden light.

As I write these words facing a deadline from my publisher, I can feel the anxiety lessening, my confidence building as I picture myself yoked with Jesus. The burden is lighter because the load is shared. I am not in this all by myself; I'm going shoulder to shoulder with Jesus, and that makes a huge difference.

A few months ago my wife and I were carrying a dresser into our home and that particular piece of furniture was very heavy. After about ten steps, the whole thing just got lighter. It lifted up like it was carrying itself. I looked behind me and saw that my next-door neighbor had quietly gotten under the load. He's more than six feet tall and weighs more than two hundred pounds. I thought to myself that this is what it's like when you're yoked with Jesus. The load is shared and lightened.

It is important to notice that Jesus says, "My yoke is easy" (Matthew 11:30). The yoke that Jesus has chosen for you is light and easy. The yoke you generally choose for yourself is heavy and burdensome. In the Greek the word for "easy" is better translated "form fitted." Carpenters in Jesus' day made form-fitted yokes to fit the contours of the backs of animals. Jesus is saying that His yoke is fitted especially for you.

It comes down to this. The words of Jesus in the Matthew passage offer you a rich cluster of metaphors that can help you savor a picture of God as a gentle friend walking beside you, whose singular purpose is to set you free from the heavy loads you place upon your weary shoulders. The world is looking for a God who cares about the heavy burdens we bear.

The challenge is for you to keep looking for new images, metaphors, stories or parables that give you a fresh glimpse of God, to see a previously overlooked aspect of God's marvelous nature that will cause your spirit to soar! Such a practical discipline will keep before you a Savior who is as challenging as He is captivating. God's mercies are new every morning

(Lamentations 3:23). Your privilege is to discover them one by

one and allow the wonder of God's grace and the extravagance of

God's love to fill your life to overflowing.

ACKNOWLEDGEMENTS

In "The Message of the Wesleys" there is a poignant sentence: "It cannot be that people should grow in grace unless they give themselves to reading." Books written by mature Christian authors are a vital source of sustenance for our inner life, giving us fresh and compelling images of God and a deeper understanding of scripture.

This book would not have been possible had it not been for one whose spiritual journey has also been guided and inspired by the printed word. In addition to her candid critique of this book, my wife Carole offered her enthusiastic encouragement all along the way, even when I disappeared for days at a time. I am grateful for the guidance of my son Danny for his no-nonsense appreciation for structure and clarity. Also, special thanks to Dr. James Laney, Dr. J. Ellsworth Kalas and Rev. Bob Moon for reading the manuscript and each making a statement on behalf of the book.

In terms of content, several people both cheered me on and held my feet to the fire. My brother Bill, an editor in his own right, gifted me with his revisions and in no uncertain terms convinced me that this work merited a readership. I wish to thank Judy Peterman, my administrative assistant, and Mike Staman who regularly helped me navigate the backwaters and undercurrents of Microsoft Word. I am grateful to Rev. Ronald Greer, Dr. Derek McAleer, Dr. Jay Harris, Dr. Craig Rikard, William B. Turner and Zimmie Goings for their encouragement and suggestions.

I wish to thank Kimberly Broerman for her assistance in preparing the section in Chapter Six entitled "The Flow of Grace." Kimberly is a spiritual director, retreat leader and founder of Deep Waters Center for Prayer and Exploration in Atlanta.

I am indebted to that group of artists and writers in Macon, Georgia, I was fortunate to meet with every week for several years as we celebrated over lunch "the creative endeavor." Two members of this group helped me in the preparation of this book. Sydney 'Skippy' Davis, a writer and retired columnist and editor for the Macon Telegraph, helped with her laser editing but more so, encouraged me to recognize the potential spiritual impact of this work.

Finally, I owe much gratitude to my publisher, A. Louise Staman, the guiding force at Tiger Iron Press. She has been a pleasure to work with and a constant source of creative nudges and boundless optimism. Louise unselfishly gave of her gifts as an award-winning poet, author and publisher to craft the best book possible. Thank you again, Louise.

Edwin Chase
Whitmarsh Island, Savannah

ABOUT THE AUTHOR

Picture courtesy of Les Wilkes

Edwin Chase, D. Min., is a United Methodist minister, pastoral counselor and author. After fourteen years of parish ministry, he joined the Pastoral Institute in Columbus, Georgia where he founded the D. A. and Elizabeth Turner Ministry Resource Center. A Fellow of the American Association of Pastoral Counselors, Dr.

Chase was the conference pastoral counselor in South Georgia for fourteen years. While serving as director of the Family Institute and chaplain at the Methodist Home for Children and Youth in Macon, he was a columnist for the *Wesleyan Christian Advocate,* writing on issues related to marriage and family life. In addition to having numerous articles published in magazines and professional journals, Dr. Chase was co-editor of the award winning book, *Patches of the Quilt: True Stories from a Children's Home.* He enjoys photography, fly-fishing and traveling with his wife Carole. They have three sons and four grandchildren. The Chases reside in Savannah.

For more information, navigate to http://www.EdwinChase.com or http://www.TigerIronPress.com.

"I have read Edwin Chase's book with profit because it is so clear that he believes what he has written. The book has the ring of conviction that comes from redemptive experience."

J. Ellsworth Kalas,
Senior Professor of Homiletics,
Asbury Theological Seminary

ENDNOTES

INTRODUCTION

xv "Panta means 'all things'": Lucado, *Love is a Package Deal*, 109.

Chapter 1

19 "people and circumstances": Kierkegaard, *Works of Love*, 213-219.

23 "not turn away": Ingram, "The Two Faces of Caring," *Weavings*, 2005, 24.

23 "Thaaaannk you, Jesus": Ingram, "The Two Faces of Caring," *Weavings*, 2005, 25.

23 "let your imagination soar": Ingram, "The Two Faces of Caring," *Weavings*, 2005, 25.

23 "qualified for our caring": Ingram, "The Two Faces of Caring," *Weavings*, 2005, 25.

25 "causes the darkness": Hugo, *Les Misérables*, 13.

26 "an honest man": Hugo, *Les Misérables*, 103.

26 "buying for you": Hugo, *Les Misérables*, 103.

28 "sin in silence": Kierkegaard, *Works of Love*, 268.

28 *"a mitigating explanation"*: Kierkegaard, *Works of Love,* 271.

29 "covers sin by *forgiving it"*: Kierkegaard, *Works of Love*, 273.

31 "to a drab grey": Jung, *Collected Works*, paragraph 551.

33 "disappointment with God whatsoever": Yancey, *Disappointment with God*, 182-183.

34 "a crashing disappointment": Yancey, *Disappointment with God*, 183.

34 "going into the ministry": Fonda, *My Life So Far*, 551.

35 "a heavy toll": Fonda, *My Life So Far*, 551.

36 "the pain that does come": Greer, *Markings on the Windowsill,* 31.

37 "we grieve our losses": Kelley, AAPC Lecture in San Francisco, April 24, 2004, n.p.

37 "family and friends": Kelley, AAPC Lecture in San Francisco, April 24, 2004, n.p.

38 "their will to live": Kelley, AAPC Lecture in San Francisco, April 24, 2004, n.p.

38 "a significant loss": Kelley, AAPC Lecture in San Francisco, April 24, 2004, n.p.

39 "took my son away": Thompson, *USA Today*, April 18-20, 2008, 1-2.

39 "to Lower Manhattan": Thompson, *USA Today*, April 18-20, 2008, 2.

39 "asking God for a miracle": Thompson, *USA Today*, April 18-20, 2008, 2.

39 "'a spurned friend'": Thompson, *USA Today*, April 18-20, 2008, 2.

40 "going to school": Thompson, *USA Today*, April 18-20, 2008, 2.

40 "was not angry or bitter": Thompson, *USA Today*, April 18-20, 2008, 2.

40 "in her absence": Thompson, *USA Today*, April 18-20, 2008, 2.

40 "thanks to God": Buettner, *AARP Magazine*, May/June, 2008, 88.

41 "looking out for them": Buettner, *AARP Magazine,* May/June, 2008, 88.

41"your quality of life": Buettner, *AARP Magazine*, May/June, 2008, 88.

Chapter 2

68 "your own song with enthusiasm": LeShan, *Cancer as a Turning Point*, 25.

68 "in the future": Greene, *The Power and the Glory,* 7.

70 "on my life": Gire, *Windows of the Soul*, 73.

71 "find a suitable substitute": LeShan, *Cancer as a Turning Point*, 13.

71 "patient's immune system": LeShan, *Cancer as a Turning Point*, 25.

71 "living one's life fully": LeShan, *Cancer as a Turning Point*, 24-25.

72 "who they are": LeShan, *Cancer as a Turning Point*, 109.

73 "plan for their lives": LeShan, *Cancer as a Turning Point*, 109.

73 "'a failed creative fire'": LeShan, *Cancer as a Turning Point*, 14, 67.

73 "and many died": LeShan, *Cancer as a Turning Point*, 25.

73 "happiest in your life": LeShan, *Cancer as a Turning Point*, 43.

73 "in a small apartment": LeShan, *Cancer as a Turning Point*, 43.

75 "times of great danger": LeShan, *Cancer as a Turning Point*, 43.

74 "others were drafted": LeShan, *Cancer as a Turning Point*, 44.

74 "relating and creating": LeShan, *Cancer as a Turning Point*, 25.

74 "times of great danger": LeShan, *Cancer as a Turning Point*, 44.

75 "began to improve": LeShan, *Cancer as a Turning Point*, 45.

75 "take the physical": LeShan, *Cancer as a Turning Point*, 45.

75 "stop by to see LeShan": LeShan, *Cancer as a Turning Point*, 45.

76 "was going so well": LeShan, *Cancer as a Turning Point,* 46.

Chapter 3

82 "is present in others": Kierkegaard, *Works of Love*, 211.

83 "is always therapeutic": Hill, *Journeys*, Summer/Fall, 2009, 21.

85 "Lord flung 'em": Downey, *Weavings*, 2005, 41.

86 "we can do nothing": Downey, *Weavings*, 2005, 41.

88 "power and beauty": Maclean, *A River Runs Through It* , 2.

89 "could see us now": Frankl, *Man's Search for Meaning* , 48.

90 "was beginning to rise": Frankl, *Man's Search for Meaning,* 48.

90 "move them to tears": Frankl, *Man's Search for Meaning*, 50.

91 "time or eternity": Frankl, *Man's Search for Meaning*, 23.

Chapter 4

99 "another through business": Keane, *The Atlanta Journal Constitution*, 6/23/2001, E10.

101 "saves the day": Muehl, *All the Damned Angels*, 64.

Chapter 5

115 "a negative light": Heller, *Psychology Today*, December, 1985, 24.

116 "their God creations": Heller, *Psychology Today*, December, 1985, 24.

116 "child's view of God": Heller, *Psychology Today*, December, 1985, 24.

116 "their imperfect parents": Heller, *Psychology Today,* December, 1985, 24.

117 "I think you're right": Stephens, *Please Let Me Know You, God*, 53.

121 "angry and vengeful tyrant": Yancey, *Soul Survivor*, 6.

121 "fear and respect to love": Yancey, *What's So Amazing, About Grace?* 52.

121 "from family and church": Yancey, *What's So Amazing About Grace?* 42.

122 "by being graced": Yancey, *What's So Amazing About Grace?* 42

122 "God's own Son die": Bondi, *Memories of God*, 24.

122 "her earthly father except worse": Bondi, *Memories of God,* 24.

123 "inadequate and depressed": Bondi, *Memories of God*, 31.

123 "the extent of our sufferings": Bondi, *Memories of God*, 31.

123 "than her earthly father": Bondi, *Memories of God,* 31.

124 "a God who 'actually liked us'": Bondi, *Memories of God*, 135.

124 "*felt* about God": Seamands, *Healing Your Heart of Painful Emotions*, 309.

124-125 "not sure He's concerned": Seamands, *Healing Your Heart of Painful Emotions*, 311.

125 "is really like": Seamands, *Healing Your Heart of Painful Emotions*, 309.

128 "new creation of this redemption": MacDonald, *An Anthology*, 92.

129 "few of its thoughts": MacDonald, *An Anthology*, 92.

Chapter 6

137 "That's the trap": Nouwen, *Life of the Beloved*, 26.

137 "not just for Jesus": Nouwen, *Life of the Beloved*, 26.

140 "for her child": Nouwen, *Life of the Beloved*, 30-31. The first five assertions in this block quote were written by Henri Nouwen. The scriptural references were added.

141 "their verdant faith a wasteland": Lake, *Clinical Theology*, 226-227.

141 "God and on *results*": Frank Lake, *Clinical Theology*, 226-227.

141 "a neurotic symptom": *Bridge Pastoral Foundation, 1*.

142 *they* were acceptable": Stibbe, *From Orphans to Heirs*, 129-130. Dr. Frank Lake originally used the word "Status" but Mark Stibbe later changed it to "Significance."

142 "in a Cycle of Law": Stibbe, *From Orphans to Heirs*, 130.

142 "were never enough": Frank Lake, *Clinical Theology*, 226-227.

142 "Cycle of Law in reverse": *How to Build a Great Life*, 1; Lake, *Clinical Theology*, 133, 136.

142 "Acceptance>Sustenance>Significance>Achievement": *How to Build a Great Life*, 1.

142 "sense of God's acceptance": *How to Build a Great Life*, 3.

143 "the course of his ministry": *How to Build a Great Life*, 3.

143 "so do we": *How to Build a Great Life*, 3.

144 "the Spirit and the word": *How to Build a Great Life*, 3.

147 "as the Father sees us": *How to Build a Great Life*, 4.

148 "work *through us*": *How to Build a Great Life*, 4.

Chapter 7

150 "Who is he": Schweitzer, *An Anthology*, 89.

167 "shall fell him ": Luther, *The United Methodist Hymnal*, 110.

167 "his riveting words": Yancey, *The Jesus I Never Knew*, 88.

168 "women and children": Yancey, *The Jesus I Never Knew*, 89.

168 "where he was, joy was": Yancey, *The Jesus I Never Knew*, 89.

170 "actually liked us": Bondi, *Memories of God*, 135.

172 "without his friend": Buechner, *Telling the Truth*, 37.

172 "I'll take *four*": Martin, Sermon at Mulberry Street United Methodist Church, February 8, 2009, n.p.

Chapter 8

175 "in God's love": Kierkegaard, *Works of Love*, 27.

176 "Christ will come again": *The United Methodist Hymnal*, 10, 14, 16, 18, 20.

183 "is there, yet hidden": Frankl, *Man's Search for Meaning*, 115.

184 "to change ourselves": Frankl, *Man's Search for Meaning*, 116.

185 "agonizing slow motion": Coffin, *Credo*, x.

186 "whatever lay ahead": Coffin, *Credo*, x.

Chapter 9

187 "bliss of the party": Olsson, *Come to the Party*, p.16.

188 "where I was": Olsson, *Come to the Party*, 16.

190 "to the Kingdom": Nouwen, *The Return of the Prodigal Son*, 13.

191 "in their lives": Achtemeier, *A Biblical Commentary for Teaching and Preaching, Nahum - Malachi*, 86.

Chapter 10

200 "dungeon of distrust": Manning, *Ruthless Trust,* 104.

BIBLIOGRAPHY

Achtemeier, Elizabeth. *Interpretation: A Biblical Commentary for Teaching and Preaching, Nahum-Malachi.* Atlanta: John Knox Press, 1986.

Buettner, Dan. "Living Healthy to 100," *AARP Magazine,* May/June, 2008.

Buechner, Frederick. *Telling the Truth: The Gospel as Tragedy, Comedy and Fairy Tale.* New York: Harper and Row, 1977.

Bondi, Roberta C. *Memories of God: Theological Reflections on a Life.* Nashville: Abingdon Press, 1995.

Coffin, William Sloan. *Credo.* Preface by James Carroll. Louisville: John Knox Press, 2004.

Downey, Michael. "Care-fully Letting Go," *Weavings.* 20, 5, 2005.

Fonda, Jane. *My Life So Far.* New York: Random House, 2005.

Frankl, Viktor. *Man's Search for Meaning.* New York: Simon Schuster, 1959.

Gire, Ken. *Windows of the Soul.* Grand Rapids: Zondervan, 1996.

Greer, Ronald. *Markings on the Windowsill.* Nashville: Dimensions for Living, 2006.

Heller, David. "The Children's God," *Psychology Today*, December, 1985.

Hill, E. Wayne. "Stretched Thin by Chronic Pain: Struggling for Meaning," *Journeys,* 11, 2, Summer/Fall, 2009.

Hugo, Victor. *Les Misérables, A Novel.* Tr. By Charles E. Wilbur. New York: A. L. Burt Company, 1925.

Ingram, Kristen Johnson. "The Two Faces of Caring," *Weavings*, 20, 5. 2005.

Jung, Carl G. *Collected Works*, 5, eds. and trans. G. Adler and R.F. C. Hull. Princeton: Princeton University Press, 1976.

Keane, Bil. "Family Circus," *The Atlanta Journal Constitution*, 6/23/01, Atlanta Newspapers, E10.

Kelley, Melissa. "Seeking Hope After Loss," A lecture given at the national meeting of the American Association of Pastoral Counselors in San Francisco, April 24, 2004.

Kierkegaard, Søren. *Works of Love.* New York: Harper Row, 1962.

Lake, Frank. *Clinical Theology: A Theological and Psychiatric Basis to Clinical Pastoral Care, Vol. 1,* London: Darton, Longman and Todd, 1966.

Lerner, Harriet G. *The Dance of Anger.* New York: Harper Collins, 1985.

LeShan, Lawrence. *Cancer as a Turning Point.* New York: E. P. Dutton, 1989.

Lucado, Max. *Love is a Package Deal.* Nashville: W. Publishing Group, 2002.

MacDonald, George. *An Anthology*, ed. by C. S. Lewis, London: Fount Paperbacks, 1946.

Maclean, Norman. *A River Runs Through It*. Chicago: University of Chicago Press, 1989.

Manning, Brennan. *Ruthless Trust: The Ragamuffin's Path to God*. New York: Harper Collins, 2000.

Martin, Tommy. "Grace for Today," Sermon preached at Mulberry Street United Methodist Church in Macon, Georgia, February 8, 2009.

Muehl, William. *All the Damned Angels*. Philadelphia: Pilgrim Press, 1972.

Nouwen, Henri J. M. *Life of the Beloved: Scriptural Living in a Secular World*. New York: Crossroads Publishing Company, 1992.
_____. *The Return of the Prodigal Son: A Story of a Homecoming*. New York: Doubleday, 1992.

Olsson, Karl A. *Come to the Party*. Waco: Word Books, 1972.

Schweitzer, Albert. *An Anthology*. Whitefish: Kessinger Publishing, 2006.

Seamands, David. *Healing Your Heart of Painful Emotions*. New York: Inspiration Press, 1993.

Stephens, Larry. *Please Let Me Know You, God*. New York: Thomas Nelson, 1993.

Stibbe, Mark. *From Orphans to Heirs*. Vineyard Abingdon: The Bible Reading Fellowship, 1999.

Thompson, Rick. "For Those Touched Most Deeply by 9/11: A Turning Point in Faith," *USA Today,* April 18-20, 2008, 26,153.

The United Methodist Hymnal. Nashville: Methodist Publishing House, 1989.

Unknown Author. *Bridge Pastoral Foundation: Towards Understanding Self and Others: Clinical Theology in Action: Dr. Frank Lake (1914-1982)* June 14, 2010. <http://bridgepastoral.org.uk/franklake.html,1>

Unknown Author. *How to Build a Great Life*: Section 2-Acceptance: Module 2.2- The Cycle of Grace, <http:/www.equipnet.org/servlets/DocumentDownloadHandler /156677/30891/45748/HTBAGL%202.2%20Cycle%20of%20g race.pdf, 1-2> April 10, 2010.

Weatherhead, Leslie D. *The Will of God.* Nashville: Abingdon, 1944.

Yancey, Philip. *Disappointment with God.* Grand Rapids: Zondervan Publishing House, 1988.

_____. *The Jesus I Never Knew.* Grand Rapids: Zondervan, 1995.

_____. *Soul Survivor: How My Faith Survived the Church.* New York: Doubleday, 2001.

_____. *What's So Amazing About Grace?* Grand Rapids: Zondervan, 1977.

Study Guide

GOD'S RELENTLESS LOVE

Chapter 1
LOVE ALWAYS BELIEVES THE BEST

Reflection / Discussion Questions

1. In your own words, what does it mean to believe all things concerning someone?
2. According to Søren Kierkegaard, what are the three ways love "covers" a multitude of sin and stops the multiplying process?
3. Discuss Jesus' statement in Matthew 5:42 about those who ask for money on the street.
4. Do you expect God to be loving and kind to you personally? If not, what keeps you from expecting this?
5. Do you believe that *everything* that happens comes from the hand of God? Discuss Jesus' comment about the fall of the tower of Siloam (Luke 13:4-5).
6. The author states: "The way you see God in your innermost being, as harsh and distant or kind and gracious, is a decisive factor in how well you will manage a season of grief. Discuss the research of Dr. Melissa Kelley.
7. If you carry a regret from your past, one when you did your best, how would you respond if you were told, "If you

could have done it better (at that time), you would have."
Discuss.

8.   If you are convinced that someone is worthless and
     possesses no redeeming attributes whatsoever, how would
     this affect your attempts to believe all things concerning
     that person?

Chapter 2
LOVE HOPES BEYOND ALL REASON

Reflection / Discussion Questions

1.   What new insights did you gain from this chapter?
2.   Why is it important always to connect hope with God's
     promises?
3.   Why is important that our hope be open to *all possibilities*
     and not limited to our own desires and wishes? What does
     it mean to hope in *God's time*? Discuss.
4.   When you remember with thanksgiving those times when
     God rescued you from a calamity or those times when God
     led you in a direction that was a blessing, how does that
     experience affect your faith?
5.   What two Greek words when placed together give us the
     Greek word for hope (*Elpis*)? What do these words say
     about hope?
6.   We keep hoping because we never know what God will do
     next. How were Moses and Peter surprised by God's
     unexpected actions? Discuss.
7.   Describe how hopelessness affects you.
8.   Think of a world without hope. The Apostle Paul states
     that "we are saved by hope" (Romans 8:24). How does
     hope save us?
9.   According to Dr. Lawrence LeShan, the hope of living a
     life filled with meaning and passion, the hope of doing the

work you love to do, is a hope you *cannot* live without. Discuss.

Chapter 3
LOVE ENDURES BEYOND ALL EXPECTATION

Reflection / Discussion Questions

1. Can you think of a time in your life when all you could do was to endure a situation?
2. What is it about our culture that makes it difficult to care for someone with a long-term illness?
3. How does your presence with someone in distress *always* make a difference, even when outwardly you can do nothing to improve that person's situation?
4. Speaking of her children who had squandered their lives on drugs and bad decisions, Omara, one of the Gulla grandmas off the South Carolina coast, said the following: "Sometimes ya just gotsta leave'em where the good Lord flung'em." Discuss.
5. What are some examples of enduring love found in the lives of Jesus, Moses and Paul?
6. According to Søren Kierkegaard, love builds up by presupposing love in the other person. How does this make a difference?

Chapter 4
THREE DANGEROUS DECEPTIONS

Reflection/ Discussion Questions

1. What are three subtle deceptions (the author called them dangers) that can weaken your relationship with God? Discuss each one.

2. In the parable of the householder who had gone to bed, (Luke 13:23-27) those who were rejected attempted to persuade the householder saying, "We ate and drank in your presence and you taught in our streets." What does this line of argument say about the ones rejected and their relationship with the householder? Discuss.

3. In the parable of the prodigal son, which of the two brothers do you more closely identify with?

4. For some people working hard to earn God's favor would *not* be considered a deception. Discuss.

5. How does the Pharisee depicted in Matthew 23:25 resemble the mayor in the film *Chocolat*? Do you see any of those characteristics in yourself?

Chapter 5
LOVE'S PORTRAIT DAMAGED AND REDEEMED

Reflection/Discussion Questions

1. Dr. David Seamands asserts that your thoughts about God can be very different from your "felt sense of God." Which has the greater influence on your spiritual life? Discuss.

2. How did Philip Yancey and Roberta Bondi discover a more gracious God? Discuss.

3. Do children see God as an idolized grandfather figure? What does David Heller say? Discuss.

4. What has the greatest influence on how a child will relate to others and later to God?

5. When the author asked people, "What are God's thoughts of you today?" what was the most common response? What would your response be?

6. According to George McDonald, when God reveals Himself to us, "it is in a few thoughts here and there, like small brush strokes." Discuss.

Chapter 6
LOVE'S GIFT RESTORED BY GRACE

Reflection/ Discussion Questions

1. How would your relationship with God be different if you believed that you were God's beloved son or daughter, with whom God is well pleased?
2. At the end of the section entitled "Living as God's Beloved" there is a collection of paraphrased scripture verses that describe God's thoughts of you. Some would say what is said there is too good to be true. What do you think?
3. In your own words describe Dr. Frank Lake's diagnosis of what caused the missionaries and pastors to burn out? What was Dr. Lake's remedy?
4. Where do you look for your sense of significance?
5. In what ways can you say you are bearing fruit in God's Kingdom? In what ways would you like to bear fruit? Is anything holding you back?

Chapter 7
GOD'S TRUE NATURE REVEALED

Reflection/ Discussion Questions

1. According to John 14:21, as we love and obey God, the Lord reveals or "manifests" Himself to us. Discuss.
2. Does God guide people today? Share a time when you were led by God.
3. As you reflect on the Gospel stories of Jesus, can you identify an account when Jesus acted in a way that can be thought of as likable?
4. Does God still *speak* to people today? Discuss.

5. Dr. Roberta Bondi in reading the desert monks was surprised to discover that God actually "liked us." Why do you think this surprised her? Would you have been surprised? How is God's liking you different from God's loving you?

6. Have you ever experienced a coincidence that caused you to wonder if God's hand of providence was at work?

Chapter 8
LOVE'S HIDDEN POWER

Reflection/ Discussion Questions

1. What new insights did you gain from this chapter?

2. In scripture we read that "God so loved the world that he gave his son...." How does Christ's death *for us* empower us to believe *all things* concerning people and circumstances? Discuss.

3. Read Second Corinthians 5:21: "He who knew no sin became sin in order that we might become the righteousness of God in him." According to this verse, how does God make us righteous? Can you explain Martin Luther's reference to this verse as "The Great Exchange?"

4. According to Vaclav Havel, "Hope isn't believing that we can change things; hope is believing that what we do matters." Discuss.

5. The prophetic statement: "Christ will come again," looks to the future but has a way of bending backward and touching the present moment. Discuss.

6. Dr. Viktor Frankl stated that finding meaning in a terrible situation does not make the pain go away, but makes the pain *tolerable*. Discuss.

7. In your own words describe how love on a human level finds its source in God's love?

Chapter 9: A JOYOUS CELEBRATION
and
Chapter 10: A FRESH GLIMPSE OF GOD

Reflection/ Discussion Questions

1. What is it about a feast or a great celebration that is like the Kingdom of God?
2. At work, at school, at home or at church, where do you see the signs of the Kingdom in the world today? Discuss.
3. Read the parable of the hidden treasure (Matthew 13:44) and pay special attention to the verbs. What do they suggest about our involvement in the Kingdom?
4. Have you ever lost something you valued and later found it? What were your thoughts and feelings? Discuss.
5. In the parables of the lost coin, the lost sheep, and the lost son, there is an all-out search, followed by an all-out celebration. What do these parables tell us about God and God's concern for what was lost?
6. According to scripture, the world began with a wonderful creation and will end with a great celebration. Between these two cosmic events we live in a world of evil, violence and destruction. Amid the challenges of financial crises, wars, and violence, how might the promise of the Kingdom of God coming in its fullness help you cope?
7. What are some things that can cause you to lose your focus on Jesus?
8. When you read Matthew 11:28-30, what part of that passage speaks to you?
9. Can you name some advantages of being yoked with Christ?